*Reflections on
Latin American Development*

Latin American Monographs, No. 8
Institute of Latin American Studies
The University of Texas

Reflections on Latin American Development

By Roberto de Oliveira Campos

Introduction by Benjamin Higgins

Published for the Institute of Latin American Studies
by the University of Texas Press, Austin & London

Library of Congress Catalog Card No. 67-64859
Copyright © 1967 by Roberto de Oliveira Campos
All rights reserved

Printed in the United States of America

Introduction

In April, 1964, a revolution took place in Brazil against the corruption, chaos, and creeping Communism of the regime of President João Goulart. Inflation was then gathering force with frightening speed. The high rate of economic growth that had characterized the Brazilian economy since World War II had given way to stagnation—in 1963 the per capita real income actually fell. The working class, which had managed to maintain its share of national income throughout the postwar inflation, suffered in that year a decline in that share. The balance-of-payments problem was becoming acute. Both the educational lag and the agricultural lag, so marked in Brazil, were becoming worse. President Goulart had yet to fulfil any of his promises to the people (while preaching agrarian reform he was quietly changing his position from one of the biggest to much the biggest landowner in the country); and as one source of support after another dropped away from him, Brazilians began to fear that he would be compelled to resort to a "Fidelismo" style *coup d'état* in order to stay in power. The revolution took place; Castello Branco became the reluctant President, and Roberto de Oliveira Campos was appointed as his Minister of Planning.

One of the first steps of the new government was the preparation of the Action Program for 1964–1966, which was presented to Congress in mid-August. The document was some six hundred pages long. Over three hundred pages related to individual sectors—power, transport, agriculture, industry, education, housing, natural resources, and regional development—and the rest related to general economic policies. In preparation for the CIAP Country Review, in mid-October, an enlarged and refined version was produced, in two volumes. Volume I presented the general macroeconomics, Volume II the sectoral programs plus a review of economic events in 1963–1964 and an outline of actions already taken by the government.

The basic analytical framework was straightforward: inflation in Brazil had recently reached proportions which not only brought balance-of-payments disequilibrium, but which also endangered continuous economic growth. Whatever may have been the arguments in the past regarding the effect of inflation on economic growth, by 1964 it was apparent that inflation must be checked as soon as possible, if healthy economic development were to be resumed. At the same time the government did not wish to retard growth unnecessarily nor to create mass unemployment during the transition period. Nor did it want to continue postponing, as the Goulart government had, badly needed reforms in the fields of taxation, education, land tenure, and public administration.

The government also wanted to check the process of "socialization by default"—that is, the gradual increase of the share of government in total investment resulting from inadequate investment incentives in the private sector. Accordingly, the government did not want to restrain the flow of credit to the private sector in a degree that would prevent private investment from keeping pace with the necessary minimum expansion of public investment. Certain minimum levels of investment (public and private) were needed to restore a satisfactory rate of increase in per capita income and to avoid increasing unemployment and underemployment. The state of the Brazilian economic organization is such that some investment in social overhead—especially transport, power, housing, and education—is necessary for continuing growth. Responsibility in this field has come to be assigned mainly to the public sector. When all efforts had been made to reduce current government expenses and transfer payments, a hard core of essential public outlays would remain, outlays which would be needed for economic growth itself.

The Action Program set forth five fundamental objectives of economic policy:

1. To accelerate the rate of economic growth, interrupted in 1962–1963;

2. To progressively curb the process of inflation during 1964–1965 so as to obtain reasonable equilibrium of prices at the beginning of 1966;

3. To alleviate regional and sectoral inequities and tensions created by social imbalances, through improvement of social conditions;

4. To assure, through investment policy, adequate conditions for productive employment to absorb the continuously expanding labor force;

5. To correct the tendency toward uncontrolled deficits in the balance of payments which menaces the continuity of economic development through strangulation of the capacity to import.

The revised version of the Action Program of the Brazilian govern-

Introduction ix

ment called for a progressive and programmed curbing of inflation. Monetary expansion in 1965 was to be so limited that the price increase during the year would be reduced to 25 percent. In 1966 the increase in means of payment would be held to 6 percent, equal to the projected increase in total output, so that price stability would be achieved.

The Action Program, unlike some of its predecessors, has been no "paper plan" to be discussed, shelved, and ignored. It has been the basis for action. The pace at which Congress passed the legislation called for in the Program rivalled that of the famous "hundred days" of the first Roosevelt Administration in the United States: two tax-reform bills, a banking-reform bill, housing legislation, and—perhaps most significant of all after the performance of the Goulart Administration—a sweeping agrarian-reform bill. The law is designed primarily to provide family-size farms to the masses of landless farm laborers and to those with "splinter holdings" or fragmented farms. It provides for penal taxation on large unused or underused holdings, designed to force owners of such holdings to put them to effective use or sell them off in family-size units. There is also provision for outright expropriation. But the Act is no mere "soak-the-landlord" measure; its chief aim is to raise agricultural output, and the legislation also provides for agricultural credit, extension services, improved marketing facilities, soil surveys, cadastral surveys, and other agricultural benefits. The Act reflects both the government's insistence on "stabilization, development, and reform" and the high level of technical competence of the Administration, as do the other measures taken by the Branco government.

Nor is the Program a once-and-for-all affair. The Program is regarded as a rolling one, and work on the 1965–1967 plan had begun almost as soon as the ink was dry on the earlier Program. The Ministry of Planning is also at work on a long-run plan which will provide the basis for still another, more comprehensive implementation program for 1967–1970.

By the end of 1965 the government's economic program had already produced dramatic effects both at home and abroad. The price rise of 45 percent during the year was more than the 25 percent originally projected, but a clear indication that inflation was being brought under control; the rate of price increase was only about one third of what it was when the government took over. The balance-of-payments position was greatly improved. The shock-effect of the abrupt reversal of policy brought more slow-down in investment and more unemployment than the government would have liked, but by year's end expansion was under way again and employment was increasing. Foreign investors made a tangible vote of confidence by putting hundreds of millions of new dollars into expansion or initiation of Brazilian operations. The World Bank made a loan to Brazil for the first time in six years and the International Monetary Fund provided substantial stand-by credits for the first time in several years. Brazil has become one of the really large-scale recipients of North American aid; and several European countries are also providing technical or capital assistance.

The chief architect of the Action Program was Minister of Planning Roberto Campos himself—a brilliant economist, an experienced diplomat, a development banker, and in addition a man of broad and deep culture, musician, poet, charming companion, and warm friend. As suggested in his acceptance speech when nominated as Man of the Year by the influential journal *Visão*, Roberto Campos had come a long way from his humble beginnings on the Mato Grosso frontier when he assumed the task of shaping the Brazilian economy. Campos likes to refer to himself as "a Brazilian hillbilly"; and indeed it is hard to guess what might have become of him if some Jesuit priests had not recognized the spark of genius in the small boy playing around their cloister, taken him in, and educated him as a priest. Before taking his final vows Campos recognized that his true calling lay elsewhere, but the warm humanity, deep concern for the fate of mankind, solid scholarship, and keen logic engendered by his early training have stayed with him ever since, as the essays presented below clearly show. Upon leaving the monastery he entered the Brazilian foreign service and went on to become, among other things, professor of economics at the University of Brazil, president of the National Bank for Economic Development, Brazilian representative to the General Agreement on Tariffs and Trade (GATT), ambassador to the United States, and now Minister of Planning.

Reading between the lines in some of the essays in this volume one can tell that Dr. Campos is well aware that he has chosen a lonely road. In a country accustomed to inflation for centuries, where every contract and transaction is geared to the expectation of a continuing rise in prices, only the far-sighted few could see the necessity for action as drastic as that set forth in the government's Program. The austere measures and sharp change in direction in the economy have been far from popular, and the ultimate benefits to the Brazilian people as a whole have not been immediately apparent. As the man mainly responsible for the government's economic policy Roberto Campos has borne

Introduction

the brunt of the attacks against it. He is also attacked for being excessively pro-American—his enemies refer to him slightingly as "Bob Fields," a literal translation of his name. Yet Campos is far from being uncritical of United States policy: the essays below include some sharp and penetrating criticisms of U.S. actions. Campos is not and never has been a blind adherent to an "American line." He does, however, see Brazil's future as lying with the West, and he knows that the term "American" as applied to the whole hemisphere has real content. Support for his Program is growing both at home and abroad. In some corners his name is being mentioned as a possible candidate for the Presidency.

Minister Campos' basic philosophy regarding planning and the role of the state in economic development emerges clearly from the essays published in this volume. For example, he makes a distinction between the "pragmatic" and the "romantic nationalists." Of the latter he says, "many of them, though they do not confess it, favor the dangerous surgery of revolution, while the pragmatic nationalist seeks to operate within the frame of democratic institutions and prefers reform to revolution." He adds,

I shall continue considering myself a pragmatic nationalist. I renounce the temptation of mobilizing resentment in order to gain the authority to plan development. I would rather strengthen the national entrepreneur than merely antagonize the foreigner. I would want the State not to do what it cannot do, in order to do what it should do. I prefer to love my own country rather than to hate the others.

Elsewhere he says of his countrymen, "We are not yet convinced of the very elementary truth that the State cannot give to the individual anything that it has not taken from the individual before."

I first met Roberto Campos in Geneva in 1960, when I had the privilege of working under his chairmanship in the International Labour Organization (ILO) Expert Group on Employment Objectives in Economic Development. During 1964 I had the still more inspiring opportunity of working in his Ministry on the completion and revision of the Action Program. I have twice had the pleasure of introducing Roberto Campos to audiences: once in Berlin to the meeting of Directors of Development Institutes, and once at The University of Texas when Dr. Campos delivered his Hackett Memorial Lecture. The lectures delivered on both these occasions are reproduced below. It gives me still greater pleasure now to introduce Dr. Campos to the wider audience of readers of this volume. Roberto Campos is clearly one of Latin America's most distinguished economists and statesmen; his views on Latin American economic development, and on United States-Latin American relations, have an interest far beyond the limits of the economics profession.

         Benjamin Higgins
         Ashbel Smith Professor of Economics
         The University of Texas

Contents

Introduction, *by Benjamin Higgins*	vii
Basic Problems of Economic Development in Latin America	3
United States—Latin American Relations	13
Problems of Government Policy and Administration in Latin American Development	45
Facts and Fantasy in Brazilian Development	56
Management, Entrepreneurship, and Economic Development	61
Social Engineering and Economic Development	67
Trade Opportunities of the Underdeveloped Countries	76
On the Need for Historical Perspective	88
The Dilemmas of Trade and Aid	98
Economic Development and Inflation, with Special Reference to Latin America	106
Some Notes on the History of the Alliance for Progress	122
Index	161

List of Tables

I.	Exports of Primary Products by Industrialized and Nonindustrialized Countries	81
II.	Price Indexes of Primary Products in International Trade	82
III.	Indexes of Trade and Prices of Primary Products	82
IV.	Coffee Prices, FOB (Spot New York)	83
V.	Terms of Trade of Coffee in Relation to U.S. Import Price	83
VI.	Dependence of Some Latin American Countries on Coffee Exports	84
VII.	Total U.S. Nonmilitary Aid to Latin American Coffee-Exporting Countries	84
VIII.	Brazil—Loss in Foreign-Exchange Revenue from Coffee Exports	85
IX.	Coffee in Brazilian Exports	85
X.	Brazil—Coffee Exports	86
XI.	Latin America—Coffee Exports	86
XII.	Colombia—Coffee Exports	87

*Reflections on
Latin American Development*

Basic Problems of Economic Development in Latin America[1]

Latin America is in the throes of social and economic change. The wind of rising expectations is blowing all over the land. The mold of the traditional society is being broken—in some cases by revolutionary change, while in others there is still hope for evolutionary fulfillment. How to deal with impending change in order to minimize violence, to preserve freedom, and to achieve a reasonable degree of social justice is our challenge.

Two main aspects of the Latin American politico-economic landscape deserve mention. The first is the antimilitary and antidictatorial political trend that started in 1954 and has recently been strengthened with the restoration of civilian democratic regimes in Argentina, Colombia, and Venezuela. This democratic resurgence is not irreversible: economic frustrations might lead to experimentation with extremist regimes of the socialist variety, whose myth and achievements cannot fail to impress many of the downtrodden masses in Latin America. This resurgence does give us a breathing spell to attempt to alleviate poverty and to achieve progress by peaceful change rather than by social convulsion.

The second aspect is the *mystique of development.* Economic development is now regarded as a consciously engineered process and not, as of old, as a creature of accident and fate. "Industrialization," "agrarian reform," "nationalism," "planning"—all are now parts of the daily jargon of Latin American life. It is with this problem that we shall now deal.

At the root of the developmental urge are complex reasons, generally described as the "revolution of rising expectations." In the social and psychological field, the development of transportation and of the media

[1] A speech given in July 1960 for the Kennecott Lecture Series at the University of Arizona.

of mass communication have awakened peoples previously resigned to the bondage of poverty to the possibility of a good life. At the same time, a much deeper understanding now prevails of the fact that, through investment and the diffusion of technology, the physical environment and the imbalance in the structure of resources can be changed in a direction favorable to growth. In the demographic field, there is the stark fact that an explosive rate of population growth may double the population of Latin America in the course of the next twenty-five to thirty years.

A change of the economic structure is also necessary to correct the excessive dependence on a narrow range of primary exports, and to find productive outlets in industry for surplus rural labor. Monopolization of foreign-trade profits in boom times and socialization of losses in lean periods were fairly typical behavior patterns in the traditional Latin American society, and both lead to economic instability and social injustice.

Stress and strain are in this yearning for development and often enough the fruits of economic progress are much better liked than the root and effort from which they grow.

Inner Contradictions of the Developmental Ideology

I shall now attempt to describe some of the inner contradictions of the developmental ideology in Latin America.

The first conflict arises from the operation of the "demonstration effect" or, rather, from the asymmetrical operation of this effect. It is easier indeed to imitate habits of consumption diffused by movies and television than it is to imitate habits and techniques of production. Hollywood, unfortunately, contaminates more than Pittsburgh does.

The result of this asymmetry is that often enough the benefits of increased production do not grow into additional investment but are channeled to satisfy consumption. While there is an intellectual realization in all of the Latin American countries that the "thrust" of the engine depends upon investment, it is found socially impossible to avoid increasing the "drag," through additional consumption. To a certain extent, to be sure, the increase in consumption, particularly in relation to durable consumer goods, may act as an incentive to production and elicit a greater effort from the laborer. By and large, however, even though the contradiction may be softened, it still persists. While, in a dynamic sense, investment and consumption in a developed and mature society are mutually reinforcing, in an underdeveloped country they are competitive.

A second inner contradiction of the development process derives from the rise of nationalism. Nationalism can and has been throughout history a potent force for development. It may increase the degree of social cohesion. It may mobilize energies and cause the acceptance of sacrifices. In many cases the "reactive nationalism," to use Rostow's expression, has led to a sense of pride in the national destiny and strengthened the will to escape poverty and subjugation.

But the efficacy of nationalism as a technique of social action varies according to the nature of the task. Historically it has played a vital role in leading traditional societies to the achievement of national independence or in promoting the coalescence of isolated regions or cities into organic unity. Once the transitional period of achieving the national unity and independence is surmounted, and the task becomes one of modernizing the economy, the irrational elements of nationalism may impede a rational organization of the effort. Nationalism then tends to become an ambivalent force.

Unfortunately some of its negative effects are only too often present in the Latin American landscape today. Emotional nationalism may create a distorted sense of pride in traditional behavior and may inhibit economic change and the absorption of foreign technology. It may lead to irrational decisions preventing a faster development of natural resources and condemning countries to a lower rate of development than might otherwise be achieved. It may be used as a device to close the door to more productive and efficient enterprises, perpetuating local monopolies. It may, finally, become associated with militarism, leading to a wasteful use of human and natural resources.

To extract the constructive mobilizing effect of nationalism in Latin America without falling prey to its intoxicating and irrational aspects is in fact one of the major tasks not only of economists but also of political scientists, politicians, and statesmen.

Groping toward a solution of this dilemma, I have suggested a distinction among three planes of action: nationalism of ends, internationalism of means, and supranationalism of markets. Once the goal of the society is set as being national economic and social development, the question of means becomes technical rather than ideological. The technique of achieving the maximum rate of investment and the maximum mobilization of resources may and usually does require a combination of national and international resources. It would be misguided and self-defeating nationalism to prevent the absorption of foreign capital and technology whenever they are the most rational means of maximizing the growth of output. Moreover, the economies of scale in modern industrial production require that the industrialization of Latin America be based on larger markets than those afforded by the individual national unit; hence the idea of supranational markets, now being embodied in the drive for common markets in the southern part of the continent.

The third inner contradiction derives from the tradition of state paternalism. This leads to premature attempts to redistribute income where it does not really exist. It takes the form of an elaborate social legislation that, though seldom implemented, remunerates seniority rather than efficiency and tends to decrease labor mobility; and that results, in commerce and industry, in a reluctance to take entrepreneurial risks without the protective mantle of the state. The basic conflict between the need for efficiency at all levels and the paternalist tradition is undoubtedly a serious factor retarding development. We are not yet convinced of the very elementary truth that the state cannot give to the individual anything that it has not taken from the individual before.

Traditional Theory and Latin American Ideology

Let us consider some salient points of the Latin American ideology of development, singling out those traits which seem more at variance with the prevalent doctrine on economic growth in the United States and in the already developed societies of Western Europe. I would not be so bold as to say that Latin Americans hold "revolutionary" and North Americans hold "orthodox" ideas, because this would be too easy a way out. One usually calls "orthodox," as Schumpeter once said, the ideas that one simply does not like.

I would mention only three elements in Latin American ideology. First, we have a bias against primary production and a correlated acceptance of industrialization as some sort of panacea. Second, a higher degree of state interventionism is accepted than is normally regarded as sound or healthy in the United States. Third, we have, in Latin America, a higher degree of tolerance for inflation and imbalanced growth.

The bias against primary production is of both sociopolitical and economic origin. Dependence on exports of primary products is regarded as having a colonial scent, particularly in those countries where foreign investments of the enclave type were made in mineral production. On the economic side, there is an ingrained pessimism concerning the long-run tendency of trade of primary exports (a trend which is held to be unfavorable), while the unhappy experience of sharp price fluctuations in a few major export products strengthens the move toward diversification and industrialization.

Even though the limitations of markets for primary production are quite real, deriving either from low demand elasticities for food products or from technological savings and displacements of raw materials, many Latin American countries unquestionably failed fully to exploit even such limited export potentialities as existed, adopting ill-considered industrialization policies based principally on taxation of exports for the subsidization of industry. More often than not, it was not the drive toward industrialization that was wrong—that was, indeed, necessary—but rather the method adopted: namely, the excessive taxation of agricultural and, in a few cases, mining exports. This has led to a peculiar gyration in the policy of most Latin American countries which tended to oscillate like pendulums between export promotion and import substitution.

The disappointment with the behavior of exports has led to an intensive effort toward import substitution. This is usually carried to a point that sharp balance-of-payment difficulties arise, due to the neglect of the export sector. The pendulum then swings in the other direction in favor of export promotion through the temporary alleviation of export taxation implied in the overvaluation of the exchange rate. But while giving an impression of untidiness, this policy of gyration is part of the stress and strain of the process of growth.

A second element of this ideology is the acceptance of a very large measure of state intervention and state planning, contrasting with the North American emphasis on private enterprise. Some of the reasons for the Latin American emphasis on state intervention are valid, others spurious. Few things, in fact, are more needed at the present time than a realistic theory of the appropriate measure of government intervention.

First among the valid reasons for a larger acceptance of government intervention is the derived nature of the development process of today's Latin America, in sharp contrast with the spontaneous growth process of the classical Western European and North American experience. The hero of the play in our case is not the aggressive entrepreneur and pioneer, nor is our development supply-oriented. Rather, it is demand-oriented, in the sense that it is the urge of the masses to increase their standard of living and consumption that prods governments into the formulation of development programs. This type of development has two consequences, an understanding of which is important for the comprehension of current problems in Latin America: it carries with it an inherently higher degree of government intervention and a greater inflationary pressure than prevailed in the nineteenth-century era of spontaneous growth.

The second valid group of reasons centers on the imperfections of the price mechanism, which are particularly serious in underdeveloped economies. These are results of the rigid market structure, monopolistic positions, and the relative immobility of capital and labor. In an economy traversing a period of rapid mutation and change, the risk factor increases, rendering entrepreneurial tasks difficult, particularly in projects with long maturation periods. Modern technology itself accentuates economies of scale and the lumpiness of investment, making some types of investment inaccessible to private savings except in mature capitalistic societies. Finally, the market mechanism may not be conducive to an equitable income distribution or to the attenuation of regional disequilibria that are bound to appear in a process of growth.

But while there are valid reasons for a different conception between Latin America and the United States of the desirable allocation of tasks to public and private enterprise, in Latin America there is, at times, a spurious emphasis on government intervention which is not based on rational grounds.

There is, firstly, the "illusion of transposition," or the idea that resources are somehow created, or real costs lowered, if the profit motive of private enterprise is replaced by the subsidy-pricing policy of public enterprise—particularly in public utilities and transportation. Secondly, the "paternalist tradition" leads to the promotion of public enterprise as a more generous employer. In fact, many Latin American governments seem to have discovered the strange secret of giving jobs without giving work. Thirdly, an "ideological bias" leads many to advocate an enlargement of the government sector as a surreptitious method of changing economic institutions from the capitalist toward the socialist models.

Both the rational and the spurious motivation for government intervention are to be found in daily experience in Latin America. It is

Basic Problems of Economic Development

important not to take a doctrinaire approach but to separate, tedious as the process may be, the wheat from the chaff.

The fourth element in the Latin American development approach is a greater degree of tolerance toward inflation and much more skepticism concerning the need for, and the possibility of, balanced growth. The tolerance toward inflation derives from the view that it may constitute a convenient and politically palatable form of taxation that reaches the wage and farm sectors otherwise inaccessible to taxation. Many Latin Americans also believe that in the initial phase of industrialization a sluggishness is inevitable in the supply reactions of some basic sectors which cannot rapidly adjust themselves to the changing patterns of demand.

Most Latin American economists are prone to interpret the developmental process as a series of disequilibrated sequences. They are in some way resigned to the cyclical-pendulum movement between export promotion and import substitution, between bottlenecks in economic and social overhead and subsequent corrective investment by the government; and they are also used to an alternation between feverish industrialization and periodic attempts to restore agricultural productivity and agricultural incentives. They are, in short, groping for a theory of the optimal imbalance as a more realistic substitute for the prudent advance on a broad front.

A Summary of Developmental Problems

Having dealt with the roots of the developmental urge, its inner contradictions, and some characteristics of the development ideology, I shall now summarize some of the crucial problems of economic growth in Latin America.

First, how should internal savings be mobilized and how should the foreign exchange needed for an acceleration of the rate of investment be obtained?

Second, how should we reduce the inefficiency of investment resulting from market limitations?

Third, how should the instability of export earnings be decreased?

Fourth, how should personnel be trained for a technological civilization and for the tasks of leadership?

Fifth, how may we improve the quality of the government?

Many of those tasks can only be met by the indigenous efforts of the

Latin American countries. In other fields, the assistance of the already developed nations can play a vital role.

The Latin Americans must thoroughly recognize that they have not done all that they can do to mobilize their own resources. Most of the countries have failed to create adequate institutions for the channeling of savings into productive uses. In many, persistent inflation has sapped the will to save. Luxury consumption by the capitalist groups in the midst of bitter poverty leads to economic waste and social bitterness. Furthermore, an excessive portion of savings has often been devoted to unproductive military expenditures. Finally, irrational prejudices often hamper utilization of natural resources.

In short, there is much that Latin Americans can do in the way of self-help, and many of our economists are now preaching the gospel of austerity as a pre-condition for aid. But, capital formation in underdeveloped countries depends also greatly on the importation of capital goods, which in the short run can be financed either through exports or through foreign loans and credits, even though in the long run only an expansion of exports assures final viability. I shall mention the controversy on loans and investments.

The Latin American countries claim that North American assistance to the development of the continent has been inadequate in size as compared to the assistance given to Europe and other areas; that it has been based on an unrealistic insistence on private investment; and, finally, that it has been based on the wrong methodological approach. While the European recovery program, for instance, was based on long-range estimates of needs in the form of country programs, the United States always insisted, in its dealings with Latin America, on a selective-project approach. In other words, the principle of "decisive involvement" of the Marshall Plan era was replaced by the principle of "minimal engagement." There is some substance, no doubt, in this criticism, although it is fair to recognize that, after failing themselves to adopt adequate financial programs, some of the Latin American countries have been only too prone to blame their difficulties on the inertia of the big brother.

How to reduce the inefficiency of investment due to market limitations is our second problem. Efforts are now being made in that direction through the establishment of two regional markets: one in Central America and the other in South America (but including also Mexico). The idea in itself is unassailable since the industrial development of Latin America, if it is to proceed on an efficient basis, must in any case

Basic Problems of Economic Development

count on markets larger than those provided by the national unit.

A third problem is the instability of export proceeds, an instability resulting from wide price fluctuations in a narrow range of exports. Selective industrialization appears to be the long-run answer for a number of countries whose markets and resource structure justify industrial diversification. But, at least in the short run, stabilization agreements hold part of the answer. The United States policy has been largely noncommittal on this line; and, only recently, it has shifted from the principle of noninvolvement to an active consideration of individual commodity problems. It is fair to recognize, however, that many of the Latin American countries have mutilated their export potentialities by the use of overvalued exchange rates for exports and ill-considered price-support policies, all based on an excessively pessimistic appraisal of exports of primary products and on an excessive enthusiasm for the financing of industrialization through the convenient but dangerous method of export taxation.

Much could be said, were time available, on tariff policies and problems since, in many cases, the instability of export earnings of Latin America has been brought about, or at least aggravated, by restrictive policies in the United States designed to protect U.S. producers through measures that throw the burden of adjustment precisely on the exporting nations which are poorest and least able to afford that burden.

The fourth problem faced in the region is the training of personnel for technological tasks and for leadership. This is an area in which the assistance of the United States and other industrialized countries promises great fruit. All who deal with development problems and inquire into development history are more and more convinced that the so-called conventional inputs—capital and labor—fall short of explaining the rapid growth of many of the industrial societies. There is an increasing conviction that the wondrous and silent operation of human capital, the laborious formation of skills that render men the most flexible and rich of the natural resources, are at the very root of the development problem. Education and training are like the two-thirds of the iceberg that remains submerged but is, in effect, much more important than what appears on the surface.

The fifth on this list of problems is the improvement in the quality of government. One of the tragedies of this era of derived development—as distinct from the era of spontaneous development—is that a larger degree of government intervention is required precisely in the countries that are least able to provide it, because of the low level of administrative skills and techniques. A vicious circle is then created: the more governmental planning and intervention is needed, the more wanting is the capacity and ability of the government and the managerial groups to undertake the task. That is one of the most serious of all development bottlenecks and is one of the reasons why many of the Latin American economists, from a formerly over-enthusiastic and naïve acceptance of state intervention, are now passing through a period of agonizing reappraisal.

United States–Latin American Relations[1]

This discussion attempts to analyze tensions—political and economic—that have arisen in the relations between the United States and Latin America from the period of the Monroe Doctrine to the new era ushered in by the Alliance for Progress. Such tensions are in part specific to this continent, reflecting the peculiarities of geographical contiguity and the interplay of political power and economic imbalance between the United States and Latin America. In part they are susceptible of generalization, reflecting issues that, in the world at large, affect the relations between a leading industrial and financial power and the less developed countries. In this area we may find the problems of economic dependence, political intervention, and the ideological issues of the cold war.

I shall start with a brief review of the long-term historical evolution of inter-American relations, discussing in somewhat greater detail the course of U.S. foreign policy in relation to Latin America after World War II. I shall then explore the several types of tension that can be identified in this review of inter-American relations, with a more detailed comment on recent sources of economic tension. I shall finally discuss the problems and outlook of the Alliance for Progress.

The Key Ideas in the Evolution of Inter-American Relations

The simplest way of reviewing inter-American relations over the last century is to pinpoint some major ideas that were the engines of either action or controversy. Those key ideas—the "ideas force" in the Hegelian sense—were (a) the Monroe Doctrine and its interpretative by-

[1] A paper submitted to the Conference on Tensions in Development in the Western Hemisphere, August, 1963, at the University of Bahia, Salvador, State of Bahia, Brazil.

products—the Polk and Roosevelt corollaries; (b) the creation of the Pan American Union; (c) the Good Neighbor Policy and its principle of nonintervention; (d) the Operation Pan America and the Alliance for Progress.

The *first master idea,* one that impregnated an entire century, was the Monroe Doctrine, contained in the President's Message to Congress on December 2, 1823, which had a forerunner in the "no-transfer resolution" of 1811. Both the Monroe Doctrine and the no-transfer resolution never ceased simultaneously to amaze and to irritate European strategists. Metternich, the most ingrained European of them all, once berated the Monroe Doctrine as "an indecent declaration." Almost a century later the German geopolitical school rated it as the most superb idea of the century, because of its principle of "nonintervention" based on the pure notion of "space" and not on historical and juridical tenets.

The Monroe Doctrine was admirably adjusted to the concept and requisites of the *defensive imperialism* which marked the beginning of the expansion of the United States as an independent nation. As the United States, having gradually tamed its territory, turned into an "extrovert power" and, conscious of its new strength, launched an extracontinental bellicose adventure against Spain, a new leading idea emerged. This was the so-called "Roosevelt corollary," which expressed itself in the policy of the "big stick." This was simply the statement of the right to "intervene to prevent others from intervening" and it can be regarded as the extreme expression of the concept of *patronizing imperialism.*

The Monroe Doctrine was a bold geopolitical gesture not based on a posture of strength. The dominant military factor in those days, which alone could enforce the Monroe Doctrine, was the British fleet which, of course, could only be counted upon to prevent encroachment by rival European powers but not to prevent intervention dictated by British interests. Thus Britain occupied the Malvinas Islands in 1833, proceeded to the annexation of Belize in 1869, shared in the French-Anglo intervention in the River Plate in 1825 and in the American-French-Spanish expedition against Mexico in 1862. In its origin the Monroe Doctrine was unilateral and nationalistic, expressing the traditional policy of continental isolationism contained in George Washington's famous Farewell Speech, but it also reflected the concern of the United States over the Russian infiltration along the Northwest coast and the interventionist policy of the Holy Alliance. None of the leading statesmen, Monroe, Adams, Clay, Polk, sought to convert it into a continental pact subscribed by the Latin American republics.[2]

Despite its nationalistic and unilateral formulation, the Monroe Doctrine was unhesitatingly accepted by the Latin American countries. Colombia and Mexico welcomed enthusiastically the new policy; and Brazil, while never resorting to its protection, has sought repeatedly, since the Fourth Inter-American Conference in Buenos Aires in 1910, to transform it from a unilateral policy declaration into a continental undertaking.

This "continentalization" of the Doctrine has come to pass only in the immediate post-World War II period, through the adoption of the Act of Chapultepec in 1945 and the Reciprocal Assistance Treaty of Rio de Janeiro in 1947.

While the Monroe Doctrine was a source of tensions in the relations between the United States and Europe, it was generally welcomed by the Latin American states. The same, however, cannot be said of some of its corollaries, which have been at the root of some of the major historical tensions in the Hemisphere. The first is the so-called "Polk corollary." In his message to Congress in 1845, after reiterating the principle of nonintervention for the purpose of barring Europe from incursions into the new world, Polk issued a warning to the effect that if a former colony, after breaking relations with the metropolis and declaring its independence, should wish to join the United States, this ought to be regarded as a "family decision." The Polk corollary was designed to prepare the ground for the accession of Oregon, Texas, and California. While in a formal sense directed mainly against Spanish intervention, it did in fact affect very deeply the interests of Mexico, the natural legatee of Spain's northern empire. The second corollary, named the "Roosevelt corollary" after its proponent Theodore Roosevelt, was to become a fuel for attrition, for it must carry the responsibility for having inspired several armed interventions in Central America and the Caribbean. It claimed for the United States the right to intervene in the internal affairs of the Latin American republics, if they did not behave with reasonable efficiency and decency in political and social matters, or if they failed to maintain international order or to meet international financial commitments.

The *second idea force* was the Pan American movement, which unfolded in two phases: (a) the Hispano-American or Bolivarian phase,

[2] G. Nerval, *Autopsy of the Monroe Doctrine* (New York: Macmillan, 1934).

embodied in the Letter of Jamaica of 1815 and the Panama Congress in 1826; and (b) the Pan American Union movement, which found expression in the invitation tendered by the U.S. Secretary of State James Blaine in 1881 for the Conference of the Inter-American States which was finally convened in 1890.

Even though in the implementation of the Bolivarian conception emphasis was given exclusively to the political and juridical problems of the Confederation of the Latin-Spanish Countries, Bolivar himself had thought in pragmatic economic terms, broaching both the idea of a single currency and that of a customs union. But the divorce between political structure and economic needs was to continue until almost our day. While the formation of a customs union was also among the main objectives of Blaine's convocation, the First Inter-American Conference in 1890 did not implement the idea, largely because of the protectionist sentiment then strong in the United States. The subsequent conferences in Mexico (1901), Rio de Janeiro (1906), Buenos Aires (1910), and Santiago (1923), were largely concerned with juridical matters and the creation of a juridical infra-structure for the system. The political phase can be said to be ushered in by the Inter-American Conference on the Consolidation of Peace which convened in Buenos Aires in 1936, and which benefited from the tension-reducing environment created by the Rooseveltian formulation of the "Good Neighbor Policy," to which we shall now turn.

The economic phase of Pan American cooperation did not really assert itself until much later with the launching of Operation Pan America, in 1958, followed recently by the Alliance for Progress.

The *third idea force* of the United States policy in relation to the Southern countries has been the "Good Neighbor Policy," with its corollary principle of nonintervention. The Good Neighbor Policy laid the foundation for a durable system of peaceful political coexistence refined in its juridical aspects, though void yet of economic substance.

During the interregnum of the Republican administration between 1952 and 1960, the Good Neighbor Policy found a revised expression in the policy of "Good Partnership," which, however, was merely an adaptation of the earlier theme to reflect the more conservative approach of the Republican Party's foreign policy.

The *fourth idea* of the Inter-American system was launched by President Kubitschek in the proposal for a Pan American Operation designed to bring to the foreground the problem of economic underdevelopment and to emphasize the collective responsibility of the Americas in its elimination. Subsequently, President Kennedy's Alliance for Progress, an outcome of and a complementation to Operation Pan America, entered the beclouded Inter-American scene. But more on this later.

Even though the pattern of North American political behavior in the one and a quarter centuries between the Monroe Doctrine and World War II may have assumed various shapes, its geopolitical underpinning centered on the continental space of the Western Hemisphere remained unchanged. In fact, throughout the Roosevelt era, even though political realities had long ago forced the United States to abandon its isolationism in respect to Europe, the Hemisphere continued to be the area of special interest or, to use a more pedantic phrase, the area of geopolitical priority.

In recent years, however, in the interval between the eruption of the cold war and the formulation of the Alliance for Progress, the geopolitical axis of the United States defense has shifted to the European peninsular area and heartland and to the maritime fringes of other continents.

The Approach of the Peninsular School

In the agitated postwar era under General Marshall and Secretary Acheson, a new approach emerged which, for lack of a better word, I shall call the *Peninsular School of Thought*. This term is appropriate because the European peninsula became the area of geopolitical priority. The crucial theme of the United States foreign policy was then to deny to the Soviets the domination of Western industry and resources, and to preserve Western Europe from contamination by the Soviet ideology.

The working concepts of the peninsular school seem to have been twofold. The first was that the attention of the United States should concentrate primarily on the areas most exposed to Soviet pressure, either because of their vulnerability to armed conquest or because of their proximity to the center of Soviet ideological contamination. Thus, during the immediate postwar period the European peninsula and the maritime fringe of the eastern Mediterranean won top priority in the American design. The second concept was that, in view of the limitation of economic resources, public investments, loans, and grants should be channeled for the reconstruction and development of those danger areas; the needs of the underdeveloped countries of Latin America, Africa, and Asia should, insofar as practicable, be met by the operation of private capital. Furthermore, foreign aid should be handled as some sort of "ideological bactericide," and injected in such fashion as to prevent an abrupt fall in the European standard of living, with the subsequent proletarization and dissolution of the middle class by subversive pressures.

This then appears to be the design underlining the Marshall and Truman Plans.

The Policy of Residual Treatment and the Perilous Lull

The United States policy in relation to its southern neighbors was throughout this period relegated to a residual position. This was the period of the "perilous lull." Viewed from the Latin American angle, this policy seemed to rest on the following premises. First, Latin America had lost priority in relative terms because its strategic importance had declined, as a result of changing concepts of warfare, and of the displacement of the area of potential contamination. Secondly, that Latin American development was a task to be left to the responsibility of private funds, supplemented by such public loans as the Export-Import Bank or the International Bank of Reconstruction and Development (IBRD) might extend after meeting urgent reconstruction claims. This interpretation, though not completely unbiased, appears justified by the course of events.

It is clear that this "residual treatment" and the reversal of the traditional priority concepts were never accepted good-naturedly by Latin American countries, even though they recognized the realities of the situation and the danger of Soviet aggression. This also explains the cool and at times hostile reaction of Latin America to the Marshall Plan, a reaction which seemed at the time shocking and disconcerting for many Americans who expected a warmer recognition of their generous and self-sacrificing approach to the problems of European reconstruction.

The issue was further beclouded by the fact that within the hemisphere the United States postwar policy suffered from a certain degree of indeterminancy, vacillating between the *principle of uniform treatment* and the *key-country approach.* Initially it seemed to adhere to a pattern of standardized behavior: maintenance of the status quo and a balanced treatment for all members of the community. Two exceptions to the rule of standardized behavior seem to have occurred. The first one was the Braden experience, which involved the application of economic sanctions against dictatorial regimes. The second, toward the end of the Acheson administration, was a brief essay in the application of the "key-country" approach. The establishment of the Joint United States Brazil Economic Development Commission in 1950 was in fact a prematurely abandoned attempt to choose a special area for a concentrated economic development effort. It had the double objective of strengthening the traditional political solidarity between the two nations through more intimate economic cooperation, and testing the workability of a program for economic development within the capitalistic framework—demonstrating its effectiveness by contrast with socialist planning.

During the transition from the Truman to the Eisenhower administrations in the postwar period, several of the postulates of the peninsular school of though became outdated.

The very success of the Marshall Plan yielded the twin result of lessening the Communist danger in Europe while widening the economic gap between North American and Western European economics, on the one hand, and the stagnant or slow-growing economies of Latin America, Asia, and Africa, on the other.

Conscious of the need for a dramatic demonstration of interest in the fate of underdeveloped countries, the United States government launched the Point-Four technical assistance program in January, 1949. This was a brilliant idea and gave considerable satisfaction to the underdeveloped areas including Latin America, which welcomed the program, viewing it as a preparatory step for an investment effort. The attendant political risk was that technical assistance sharpens the hunger for, and increases the ability to use, investment capital and, if investment programs are not forthcoming, the result might be increased disappointment.

The Neogeopolitical Approach

The most important development of recent years, however, occurring, for the most part, during the period of the Republican administration, but overlapping also the initiation of the new Democratic administration, was the abatement of ideological pressure from the Communists in Europe, its catastrophic recrudescence in Asia, and the problem created by the emergency of new nations in Africa, deeply influenced by Western culture but afflicted by resentment against colonialist domination.

In this changed scenery, new patterns of foreign policy emerged. During the Eisenhower administration the trends of foreign policy could be described as the "neogeopolitical approach." This new school of thought has geopolitical roots but those are not planted on this continent, as were those of the Monroe Doctrine, but on distant soils. The fact is that, whether the Latin Americans like it or not, geopolitical postulates themselves have changed *pari passu* with the assumption of world leadership by the United States. The problem was no longer to deny Western European countries access to the continental preserve. It was rather to maintain the influence of Western ideas in Asia and the Middle East and in the newly emerging countries in Africa. It is to prevent the ideology that now rules over the Eurasian heartland from taking hold of the maritime fringes of the Middle East and Asia, the Far Eastern lands, and the Indian subcontinent, as well as of the emerging countries of Africa.

It is thus that the NATO organization came to be supplemented by SEATO and that the Marshall-Plan effort has been replaced by substantial aid programs (often interrupted by political strife) for the Middle East and Asia.

From the Latin American viewpoint, the approach of the neogeopolitical school presented no special merits over its predecessor, except perhaps that it placed the United States in more direct contact with the stark realities and the anguishing problems of economic backwardness. The experience thus acquired could be useful in handling the Latin American underdevelopment problem, which is basically simpler and more readily tractable than that of some of the lands of Asia, the Middle East, and Africa.

The Pluralistic Approach of the New Frontier

Until 1958 there had been no change in the residual treatment allotted to the Latin American countries in the United States postwar economic policy. This was the era of the "perilous lull," from which there was a rude awakening under the impact of two shocks: the *Nixon incident* in May 1958 and the *Cuban revolution* in 1959. The first shock, which induced a policy reappraisal, arose when incidents during the Nixon visit to Venezuela and Peru in 1958 brought dramatically into the open the grave disintegration of Inter-American relations. This incident created the opportunity for the launching by President Kubitschek of Brazil of the idea of Operation Pan America, a much-needed reappraisal of the state of relations between the United States and Latin America.

Although Operation Pan America was received in the United States with only surface cordiality, it did stir a new trend of thinking, leading to a revision of long-standing behavior patterns in United States foreign policy, and ultimately to the formulation of the Alliance for Progress. The latter was actually born under the impact of urgency and the stress on social reforms arising from the Cuban revolution. If we trace from 1958 the main steps of the revision, we note the following chain of events: (a) the declaration by Mr. Douglas Dillon, Under Secretary of State, in August, 1958, of the intention of the United States to acquiesce to the creation of the Inter-American Development Bank, an old-standing aspiration present at most of the Inter-American economic conferences of the last fifty years; (b) President Eisenhower's "Newport Declaration" of July, 1960, in which he announced the United States' readiness to give financial assistance for social-development programs if the Latin American countries would undertake some necessary institutional reforms; (c) the Act of Bogota, precursor of the Alliance for Progress, in which the Latin Americans committed themselves to undertake reforms in land structure, taxation, housing, and education, while the United States promised financial assistance for social progress;[3] (c) the launching, on March 13, 1961, under a new Democratic Administration, of the scheme of the Alliance for Progress, later to be multilaterally subscribed, on August, 1961, at the Conference of Punta del Este.

The inception of the Kennedy administration was marked by a broader approach which might be termed the "pluralistic" view of foreign policy. In many cases the new approach was merely the culmination of changes already in the offing during the latter part of the Eisenhower administration; in others it represented a major departure

---

[3] This promise was implemented through the appropriation by the United States Congress at the inception of the Kennedy administration of $400 million for social development projects, of which $394 million were turned over to the Inter-American Development Bank for multilateral administration. This succession of steps in policy revision is well described in a speech given in Philadelphia on May 24, 1962, under the title, "The Alliance for Progress at the City of Philadelphia," by Mr. T. Graydon Upton, executive vice-president of the Inter-American Development Bank.

from traditional behavior. In addition to a substantial revision of the attitudes in relation to Latin America, which is manifest in the launching of the Alliance for Progress, the "pluralistic" foreign policy can be said to have the following main characteristics. (a) A more pragmatic attitude prevails regarding neutralism, contrasting with the moralistic view of the problem in the Dulles period in the State Department. Thus, neutralism in certain areas of border tension has come to be recognized as an acceptable, if not ideal, posture. Greater emphasis is laid on the pursuit of independence by the underdeveloped countries than on alignment with the Western world. (b) A much deeper engagement in the promotion of economic and social advancement of the less developed countries has become of basic priority in the United States foreign policy; simultaneously a much less inhibited support is given to the liquidation of colonialism, an objective hitherto pursued cautiously because of the United States' involvement in European alliances. (c) Foreign assistance is used more boldly as a leverage instrument to press for institutional and fiscal reforms, even at the cost of antagonizing governmental and social structures regarded as obsolete. (d) Greater acceptance is shown of institutional pluralism in underdeveloped countries, in recognition of the fact that during the transition from colonialism to independence, and in the drive for modernization of the societies, authoritarian democracies, mixed socialist systems, and a substantial degree of government planning and orientation of the economy may be useful to accelerate structural transformation. Correlately less emphasis is placed on the role of private enterprise and the pre-emptive role of foreign investment.

Sources of Tension in Inter-American Relations

After this historical interlude we should now review the major sources of tensions in the relations between the United States and the Latin American countries.

In a classification which is not comprehensive and does not purport to be *valuational* (that is, does not involve a value judgment, at this stage, on the positive or negative aspects of the tensions) the following sources of tension—some of historical, some of current relevance—may be listed:

1. Reactive tensions
2. Ideological tensions
3. Racial and cultural tensions

4. Institutional-reform tensions
5. Economic disputes

The Reactive Tensions

The *reactive tension* has its roots in deep-seated resentments against (a) geographic mutilation, such as that imposed on Mexico, by the annexation of California and Texas, or on Colombia through the fostered secession of Panama to facilitate the building of the Canal; (b) armed intervention and occupation in Nicaragua (1912/1933), Mexico (Vera Cruz, 1914), Haiti (1915/1934), Dominican Republic (1916/1924), Costa Rica (1919); (c) political intervention, such as the special rights reserved to the United States under the "Platt amendment" to the Cuban constitution, enacted in 1901 and abrogated only in 1934; and (d) economic domination, through the overwhelming influence exercised in the past by American private interests, such as the oil companies in Venezuela, the United Fruit Company in Central America, the sugar interests in Cuba.

While the United States policy in Latin America, particularly since the Good Neighbor Policy and the Rio de Janeiro Reciprocal Assistance Treaty, has moved in the direction of collective action in lieu of unilateral intervention, and the strength and influence of private companies has yielded in the face of stronger local governments and nationalist reaction, tensions still lurk below the surface. This explains the morbid sensitivity of Latin America to United States' intervention even when in individual cases there may be basic sympathy with its objective—such as the toppling of an archaic dictatorial regime in the Dominican Republic or the containment of the Communist threat in Cuba.

Ideological Tensions

The second major source of tension, linked mainly but not exclusively to the outbreak of the cold war, is *ideological* in nature. Such are the issues posed by Communist infiltration, nationalism, neutralism, and the "policy of independence."

Communist influence in Latin America is a major source of tension in the relations between the United States and Latin America, particularly because of its rather successful effort to instill in the indigenous nationalist movements an obsessive anti-Yankee fixation. Although the Marxian doctrine—preaching that international solidarity of the workers' movement and internal class struggle within each country is essentially antinationalist—the pragmatic adaptations made by Lenin for the creation of Russian socialism, and particularly the Maoist revisionism, which replaces the emphasis on internal class struggles by the emphasis on national anticolonial movements (enlisting the support of the petit bourgeois and national capitalist groups) greatly facilitated the infiltration by the Communists of nationalist movements in Latin America. The latter were then distorted into an anti-United States nationalism, a relatively easy distortion in view of historical resentments and other tensions arising from the economic and political imbalance between the colossus of the north and its weaker neighbors of the south.

Quite apart from the spurious marriage between nationalism and Communism, there are several strands of the nationalistic movement in most Latin American countries that are also tension increasing. They are, to use Mario Henrique Simonsen's[4] expression, the "phantasmagoric" and the "monopolistic" variants of nationalism.

Nationalism

Phantasmagoric nationalism rebels against colonialism when colonialism is on the decline the world over and was never relevant, in its traditional form, in the relations of the United States with Latin America. Economic imperialism from the north is blamed for the evils inherent to conventional colonialism and singled out as a target for nationalist tensions.

Another variant of phantasmagoric nationalism is the opportunistic nationalism through which unscrupulous politicians maneuver to divert the people's attention from the real cause of underdevelopment and seek solace from the frustrations of underdevelopment by transferring the guilt to foreign scapegoats.

Monopolistic nationalism is generally fostered by the so-called "industrial progressives" (or the "national capitalists" to use terms of the Maoist revisionism), which seek to use nationalism as a device to preserve national monopolies and stave off foreign competition, not only by the traditional mechanism of tariff protection, but also by creating an investment climate inimical to entry or survival of foreign invest-

[4] Mario Henrique Simonsen, "Tension in Underdeveloped Countries" (background paper for "Tensions in Development in Western Hemisphere"), pp. 11 and 12.

ment in local industries. In view of the dominant trade and investment position of the United States interests in Latin America, monopolistic nationalism seeks to mobilize public opinion against "foreign" (that is, American) monopolism.

Independently from those aberrations, however, the very emergence of nationalism throughout Latin America is bound to create a certain amount of tension. This is because several of the components of the nationalist ideology—which is far from constituting a coherent body of thought—run counter to prevalent beliefs and accepted tenets in the already industrialized nations, and particularly in the United States, as indicated by the following characteristics which, according to Marcilio Moreira, can be pieced together from disconnected strands of the nationalistic thought in Latin America.

1. Industrialization is given absolute priority. To develop is practically identified with to industrialize.

2. Heavy reliance is placed on the state as a direct entrepreneur.

3. The export of raw materials is generally considered humiliating, and in certain cases the export of minerals as especially degrading because it robs the nation of an unsubstitutable wealth.

4. Foreign private capital is distrusted particularly for direct investment or for the exploration of natural resources or public utilities. This suspicion does not apply, however, to capital in the form of loans, either private or public, a form of financial cooperation that usually is welcomed or even eagerly sought.

5. Over-all planning by the state is considered necessary. This belief is only of a general nature and often is not translated into a policy, even less into technical decisions.

6. Agrarian reform is considered necessary, but merely as an instrument of social justice or as a purely ideological "must." The factors of increased agricultural productivity are usually undervalued.

7. The "nationalism movements are often imbued with a high distrust of the 'balance-your-budget ideology' and favor a 'structuralist' interpretation of inflation and development."[5]

The recrudescence of nationalism seems disconcerting at a time when Western Europe and the United States are seeking to escape the confines of nationalism in a search for broader forms of supranational in-

---

[5] Apud Marcilio Moreira, "Some socio-political preconditions of Economic Growth" (Unpublished M.A. thesis, Georgetown University, Washington, D.C., April, 1962), p. 96.

tegration and interdependence. But this must be viewed in a historical perspective; if it is so interpreted, undue tensions need not arise.

The Western industrialized countries have, by and large, completed their process of national and social integration. The only major remaining pressure is the external threat of Communist aggression, against which the best defense lies in supranational integration. The Latin American countries, on the other hand, are still in the process of constituting their national personalities. They need a cohesive force such as that of nationalism, to maintain unity against the centrifugal pressure of heterogeneous regions and groups, and to abate interclass tensions. In this context, nationalism may still be an important mobilizer of the national effort and a vital element in the drive for modernization—though, of course, like most ideologies, fraught with the danger of ideological perversion. It is in fact a major task of social dynamics in Latin America to utilize the mobilization potential of nationalism without falling prey to its intoxicating perils. Very often the politicians' need for political excitement and for transferring guilt may channel nationalism into irrational detours, and may hamper development itself by adversely affecting the flow of investment funds. But if a prudent and sober view is taken of this phenomenon, if the legitimate historical grievances are recognized, if account is taken of emotional urges inherent in periods of quick transformation of dependent economies into proud self-reliant nations, we shall find that nationalism in Latin America, just as in Europe, where it was first born, may give ground to more balanced attitudes, once the process of modernization is advanced and a greater degree of social integration reached.

Foreign Policy

Another possible source of tension lies in the foreign-policy field. The United States as well as Western Europe is likely to find a growing urge in the Latin American countries for an *independent foreign policy*, reflecting both the need of those countries to assert their national personalities and their different interpretations of cold-war issues. It is altogether too simple, however, to dismiss the policy of independence, which is being spearheaded by Brazil and Mexico, as just another manner of *neutralism*, or an exhibition of pro-Castro feelings. For, in fact, the independence policy of the Latin American countries differs substantially from Afro-Asian neutralism. Firstly, they are not systematically nonaligned, since they remain faithful to the Inter-American system. Secondly, they do not show interest in the formation of a third power bloc, symmetrically distant from the two big centers of power. Thirdly, they have chosen Western institutions of representative democracy and capitalism, even though practicing them imperfectly, while the typical neutral country has not yet crystallized its choice between democracy and private enterprise on one hand and authoritarian socialism on the other.

The cold war is also viewed differently. For the Western industrialized nations, the overwhelming problem is to protect their tested and workable institutions from the external Communist threat. For Latin America there is yet another chasm just as relevant as the East-West conflict. It is the abyss that separates them from the prosperous industrialized countries of the Northern Hemisphere. The Western industrialized countries, for which external aggression is the only relevant threat, tend to view the cold war as a problem of security; the Latin American countries faced with internal threats of poverty and dissatisfaction are less concerned with external security than with internal development.

It is thus no wonder that those countries, while conscious of their basic solidarity with Western ideals, view the cold war from a different perspective, and are readier to accept the competitive coexistence of the two systems. This is not only because coexistence seems the only viable alternative to global holocaust or to a rigid partition of the world in ideological compartments, but also because they believe that the competition with socialism will render democratic capitalism more humane and socially conscious and, as an incidental by-product, may prod the West into greater efforts, with a greater sense of urgency, in helping underdeveloped areas.

The Problem of Fidelismo

All of the foregoing sources of tensions found a powerful condenser in the "Fidelist" revolution. It plays on the nationalist theme by mobilizing traditional resentments, particularly strong in Central America and the Caribe, against U.S. intervention and economic domination. It harps on the ideological ways of Communism with its emphasis on correction of social inequities and accelerated development through planning. It caters to the Latin-American pride by asserting the national personality of a small country against a powerful neighbor.

It is thus no wonder that *Fidelismo* has become a major breeder of tensions in the Hemisphere. Its appeal cuts across geographical frontiers and permeates several strata of the population. For the intellectual and professional groups the main allure is the "mystique of growth" and the magic appeal of collectivist planning as a short cut to development. To the broad masses the appeal lies in the promises of redistributive justice and in the courageous break with the existing social order.

The tensions generated by the Fidelist movement affect not only the relations of Latin America with the United States but also the relations among the Latin American states themselves. For under the compulsion of the expansionist Marxian ideology, Castro has spared no effort to infiltrate neighboring countries and to spread subversion not only against traditional oligarchic governments but against progressive governments of the moderate left. He managed effectively to divide the inter-American scene, bringing about the emergence of tensions unknown heretofore, such as the split vote at the Conference of Punta del Este on the handling of the Cuban problem. The countries more directly exposed to infiltration and subversive propaganda advocated strong action, while Mexico and five of the southern countries—for traditional reasons (the principle of nonintervention), juridical reasons (imprecision of the juridical instruments of the OAS to deal with new forms of cold-war aggression), or pragmatic reasons (fear of aggravating domestic tensions or skepticism regarding the effectiveness of sanctions)—followed a more moderate course, while joining in the condemnation of Castro's allegiance to the Soviet bloc as incompatible with the inter-American system.

Though still important as a source of tension, *Fidelismo* has lost some of its original luster. The appeal to nationalistic sentiment in Latin America and the pride of asserting independence vis-à-vis the United States was sapped by growing evidence of submission to the social and political patterns and foreign policy of the Soviet. The unabsorbed complexities of socialist planning failed to provoke a miracle of rapid growth: the agrarian reform, based on collectivization of land rather than on its redistribution, failed, as it has elsewhere, to solve the food problem, for it did not yield the production stimulus which has been so successful in the redistributive experiments of land reform in nonsocialist countries. In this whole context, the ideological repression of the police state, which might be accepted as a price for rapid social reform and regimented economic growth, has become a grave social irritant.

Finally, by promising an alternative and more humane road to social reform and economic development, the Alliance for Progress, though yet untested by performance, is beginning slowly to erode the Castro myth. But the Castro revolution has not so far exhausted its vigor and resourcefulness as to allow us to pass on it a verdict of ineffectualness, nor has the Alliance for Progress proven its mettle. This then is the great confrontation of the next few years with its tensions, perils, and promises.

Racial and Cultural Tensions

While it is easy to exaggerate the importance of differences in racial composition and of the basic divorce between Anglo-Saxon and Latin cultural forms, as sources of tension, it remains true that those factors cannot be neglected. There is little doubt, however, that they are declining in importance. With the advance of the process of racial integration in the United States there has been an abatement of the racial discrimination against nationals of some Latin American countries, particularly those of Mexico, in the United States, thus narrowing this source of tension.

The cultural divorce is also narrowing because the very process of economic development is bringing about a faster rate of absorption in Latin America of modern technology imported largely from Anglo-Saxon sources, and also because there is an increasing store of knowledge in the United States of the language and cultural patterns of Latin America.

The Institutional-Reform Tension

Tensions may arise from attempts by the United States to influence the political systems and/or to promote or stimulate reforms in the institutions of its neighbors from the south. Those tensions may be classified according to either *means* or *objectives* into three groups.

Armed Pressure Used to Affect Political Systems

Most of the armed interventions "to restore civil order" in the Central American Republics and in the Caribbean from 1912 to 1934 had as one of their implied objectives the discouragement of dictatorial regimes, although in a good many cases the more pragmatic reasons of protecting United States property and assuring financial solvency were dominant. More recently, the military and logistic support for the overthrow of the Arbenz Guatemalan regime and assistance in the

Cuban invasion, as well as the display of naval force in Santo Domingo to prevent the restoration of the Trujillo family rule, exemplify attempts to induce the modification of authoritarian systems—of the left and of the right—by military pressure.

Economic Pressure Used to Enforce Canons of Monetary Stability and Fiscal Discipline

Throughout the postwar period, the U.S. government has repeatedly sought, either bilaterally or through the International Monetary Fund (in the latter case with the support of Western European countries which have in fact become lately more rigid and uncompromising than the United States), to utilize the leverage of economic and financial assistance to induce the adoption of "sound" fiscal, exchange, and monetary policies in underdeveloped countries.

It is unquestionable that this apparently reasonable linkage of financial assistance to requirements of "sound" monetary and fiscal behavior, either in bilateral negotiations or through the intermediary of the International Monetary Fund, has been a major source of tension, which reached an explosive point when Brazil interrupted discussions with the Monetary Fund in July, 1959. Here again the Latin American behavior is ambivalent since inside the countries themselves there is a sharp policy clash between the *monetarists* who would be inclined to accept the validity of monetary discipline as a means to attain an effective utilization of resources, and the *structuralists* who believe that the inflation problem in Latin America is institutional and structural in nature and cannot be curbed except through gradual actions, based on investment programs supported by foreign assistance and on institutional adaptations designed to increase supply flexibility.

While there is merit and heat on both sides of the argument, the fact is that frequently the rigid subordination of monetary assistance, particularly in the form of balance-of-payments loans, to the approval of programs of monetary stabilization and the demonstration of performance, creates a vicious circularity. This is because the monetary authorities do not operate in a political vacuum. Sound plans for combating inflation may often find political obstacles that only slowly can be surmounted. This is likely to be the case when, during the early phases of stabilization, distortions have to be corrected by letting subsidized prices rise, by allowing the exchange rate to depreciate, or by causing marginal industries to wither through credit restrictions—all of which may painfully affect large groups of people who are able to mobilize political power. Or else, the instability of export prices of primary products may play havoc with stabilization programs by rapidly cancelling out the borrowed exchange resources or decreasing tax receipts. In these circumstances, a rigid and intolerant attitude, which insists on undeviating performances in an adverse political context, may further weaken the hand of those who fight for monetary stability. It may entail ultimately a retrogression in financial and fiscal policies, and may compound the evil by restraining growth without achieving price stability, until, later, a much greater financial involvement has to be accepted under semicatastrophic or emergency conditions.[6] In recent years this has been an only too frequent experience in Latin America. Certainly, a much more sophisticated handling of this problem is called for on the part of the United States financial authorities, the International Monetary Fund, the World Bank and, last but not least, the Western European governments which, absorbed in the problems of the Common Market or of their African and Asiatic associations, have maintained either an indifferent or a rigidly orthodox position in dealing with Latin American finances.

Foreign-Aid Programs Used to Promote Basic Institutional and Structural Reforms

As a means of reducing the level of tensions while at the same time promoting political change and institutional reforms on Latin America, the United States has sought consistently throughout the years to utilize multilateral mechanisms or to get agreement from the Latin American countries on the reforms desired. Thus, in the political field, the principle of representative democracy has been written both into the Charter of the OAS and into financial cooperation programs, such as the Act of Bogota and the Charter of Punta del Este. Similarly, the requirement of basic structural reforms was made an integral part of the compact of the Alliance for Progress.

[6] Professor David Felix notes that to maintain a consistently orthodox set of economic policies against strong redistributive pressures, dictatorial governments are usually required. "It was the error of the Eisenhower administration," he says, "in its zeal to promote economic orthodoxy and a favorable investment climate, to become too closely identified with unpopular dictatorships" ("The Alliance for Progress, the Long and the Short View," *Centennial Review*, Vol. VI, No. 3, p. 325).

Latin American Attitudes

The analysis of the tensions of institutional reform presents tantalizing problems due at times to inconsistencies in the United States behavior but more frequently to the ambivalent position of the Latin American states themselves. In the political field, for instance, despite widespread disapproval of totalitarian regimes operating in violation of the principles of the inter-American system, there is hesitation and fear when pressure is applied by the United States to concrete cases, such as the toppling of the Trujillo dictatorship or the military coup in Peru. Thus the traditional fear of intervention leads Latin American countries to the contradictory attitude of denouncing totalitarian regimes but refusing to support concrete steps to discourage their implantation; or, after blaming the State Department for supporting dictatorial oligarchies, recoiling disapprovingly when the United States takes the opposite position of mobilizing economic and political pressure for the effective defense of the principle of representative democracy.

The institutional-reform tensions arising from the bold program of social transformation envisaged in the Charter of Punta del Este— land, fiscal, educational, and housing reforms—are still of a different nature. They are in a way "consented to," since by subscribing to the Act of Bogota and the Charter of Punta del Este the Latin American countries accepted those tensions as unavoidable in the process of promoting structural transformation. But while many of the governments gave formal consent to those unquestionably valid reform objectives, they may find it difficult in concrete cases to mobilize enough popular support to overcome the entrenched interests of politically powerful groups, while in a few instances the acceptance of the Punta del Este objectives may have been both less than sincere and increasingly eroded by the realization of a practical divorce between the interests of the traditional ruling groups and the egalitarian and distributivist aspirations embodied in the Charter.

Economic Disputes

Throughout the post-World War II period—marked by phases of the United States foreign policy previously described as the "peninsular approach" and the "neogeopolitical approach," during which the treatment given to Latin America was in a sense "residual"—several issues arose in the economic dialogue between the United States and its

United States—Latin American Relations

neighbors to the south. Many of those sources of tension have recently abated, largely because of a substantial evolution in the United States attitude as exemplified by the Act of Bogota and the Punta del Este Charter, but it may be useful to review them briefly.

Lending Policies

The United States adhered, practically until the signing of the Act of Bogota, to the concept of restricting foreign lending to the imported components of economic-development projects, while Latin Americans pleaded for more flexibility in order to permit the financing of social overhead projects in the housing, education, and health fields, and also the coverage through foreign lending of the local cost components of investment projects.

Finally the Latin American countries emphasized the need for flexible loans of the "soft" variety, a principle which before Bogota and Punta del Este had been only reluctantly accepted through the establishment of the International Development Association (IDA, a subsidiary of the World Bank) and of the Development Loan Fund.

Financial Mechanisms

The Latin Americans proposed on several occasions over the last half century the creation of a specialized inter-American financial institution, over whose policies they would enjoy substantial influence and which would concentrate on the problems of the area. Only in 1958 did the United States accede to the idea which materialized in the foundation of the Inter-American Development Bank, in April, 1959.

Commodity Prices

The Latin Americans laid great emphasis on the need to stabilize commodity prices, on parity schemes linking prices of primary products to those of manufactures, in order to prevent terms of trade from deteriorating, and on international cooperation through commodity agreements or compensatory financing, designed to regulate the market and/or assure stability of foreign-exchange earnings.

Until recently the attitude of the United States was sympathetic to studying the problem, but noncommittal as to action.[7] The policy was

[7] In the Inter-American Economic Conference of Finance Ministers of Petropolis (Brazil) in October, 1954, a Latin American proposal to stabilize raw-material prices was rejected by the United States as a "threat to free enterprise."

substantially modified since the Bogota Act and the Charter of Punta del Este, leading to a more active United States' participation in the effort to stabilize coffee prices, to formulate programs for the creation of funds for compensatory financing, and finally to press the Europeans for adoption of more liberal and nondiscriminatory trade practices in relation to Latin American products.

Private Investments

It may be recalled that throughout the period of "residual treatment," the main responsibility for cooperating in the economic development of Latin America was ascribed to private capital, while official financing agencies would exercise only a complementary role. This on the grounds that private investment is guided by productivity criteria and not by political or social considerations; that it carries a built-in contribution of know-how and organizational experience in those cases when it takes the form of direct private investment; and that it has a much larger reservoir of capital than public funds have, and one that is not subject to budgetary vicissitudes.

Public Investments

Latin Americans, on the whole, tend to assign a much larger function to public capital, at least in the initial stages of development. The argument proceeds thus: (a) the most urgent need at this phase of their growth is for investment in the creation of the *economic* and *social overhead,* a task usually unattractive to private capital; (b) private portfolio investment has practically disappeared, while direct investment though involving no rigid debt obligations tends to be burdensome in balance-of-payments terms, because it requires enough remuneration to attract funds in competition with profitable domestic investments within the United States or in the Common Market area; (c) paradoxically as it may seem, public loans are held to involve much less danger of political attrition than the presence, within the country, of big private investors; (d) finally, private investment is subject to imponderables—psychological, political, and economic—that cause its flow to be uneven and erratic, thus rendering difficult the formulation of development plans and programs.

Further developing a trend of thinking which was already discernible in Eisenhower's Newport Declaration and in the Act of Bogota, the Kennedy Administration took a more flexible view. While stressing the importance of private capital, it recognized, nevertheless, the validity of the insistence of Latin Americans on the assignment of a larger role to public funds, because of the nature of the investments urgently needed—economic and social overhead projects; because of the erratic behavior of private capital and its susceptibility to short-term political shocks; and because of the "vicious circularity" problem. The expansion of private investment requires an improvement of the investment climate in terms of political and monetary stability which, in turn, would presuppose a rise in the level of investment; if unable to count on adequate foreign assistance, the government would endeavor to raise the level of investments by inflationary means, thus further impairing the investment climate.

This shift of the main responsibility for financing Latin American development from private capital to public funds has been expressly set forth in the Punta del Este Charter which says in its Title II, Section 4: "The greater part of the sum (a supply of capital from all external sources of at least $20 billion in the next ten years) should be in public funds."

While there has been a great and realistic conceptual improvement through the realization of the limitations of private financing, some points of friction remain, of which two deserve mention: (a) the policy of the Washington financing agencies in refusing to lend for state oil monopolies in Latin America; (b) the controversy over expropriation of United States properties.

With regard to the first of these problems the United States policy, though never completely clarified, appears to have evolved from a complete denial of public loans for state oil enterprises, to restricted financing of certain phases of the operation (transport, refining, and distribution) for state companies of countries that allow also the functioning of private enterprises in prospecting and refining (Argentina, Bolivia), and preferably in joint investment schemes with private capital. There appears to be no restriction, however, to the financing of research and development of nonconventional petroleum sources such as bituminous shale. The alleged rationale for the policy of restrictive public lending in the petroleum field is the availability of private capital, which would justify husbanding scarce public funds for those investments that are unattractive for private capital; this contention is disputed by some of the Latin American countries, which point to the unreliability of investment decisions by the private oil companies; their lack of interest in opening up new fields of production that might compete with excess capacity owned elsewhere; the subordination of their exploration and pricing policies in Latin America to their world-wide market interests; and, finally, the political unadvisability of foreign private operations in a field of strategic importance.

The other source of controversy is the expropriation of United States properties in Latin America. This trend toward expropriation has been exarcebated by the Cuban wholesale nationalization of foreign companies, but was present in varying degrees in most Latin American countries even before the Cuban experiment. The fields most vulnerable to the expropriation drive are public utilities, public-transport systems, and oil production and processing facilities. Unlike the petroleum field, where the drive for nationalization is basically political—the desire to retain for the state control of sectors of strategic importance to the economy—in the case of transportation and public utilities there are real technical problems related to the near impossibility of private operation of tariff-regulated fields in periods of prolonged and sharp inflation. The lag of tariffs behind cost (prompted either by political demagoguery or by the sheer administrative complexities of frequent rate revisions) deter private investment, leading to deterioration of the services and creation of bottlenecks that, in turn, aggravate the political opposition to rate increases and generate public clamor for state intervention, particularly in the case of foreign enterprises targeted by nationalistic pressure.

State intervention does not of course solve any of the technical problems arising from inflation (often it increases real costs and decreases efficiency), but it does permit the continuation of investment by dividing the burden of financing between the direct user and the general taxpayer.

The "expropriation controversy" does not concern the right of expropriation itself which is unquestionably accepted both by the United States and Latin American countries as a matter of sovereignty. It refers rather to the economic wisdom of allocating resources for absorption of existing operations rather than for new investments; the determination of what is "fair and adequate compensation" both in terms of method of valuation of the properties and *currency of payment*; and the degree of acceptable diplomatic action by the government of the investor countries for the protection of the interests of their expropriated companies abroad. On the question of compensation, the usual inclination of the private investor is to resort to "reproduction costs" as the method of valuation and to require prompt payment in convertible currency, a requirement which if strictly interpreted would in fact impede expropriation, in view of the financial stringencies of most Latin American countries both in terms of fiscal resources and foreign-exchange availabilities. The tendency of the Latin American countries on the other hand is to advocate the payment of compensation in installments, a major proportion being paid in local currency independent of convertibility provisions, and often with tied-in reinvestment clauses. With regard to the degree of diplomatic protection, the position of the Latin American countries is generally that only in the case of denial of justice by local courts does the problem become a legitimate case of "protection of nationals" under international law. As long as internal legal remedies have not been exhausted, diplomatic protection is regarded as improper.

In practice the United States government has, on the whole, taken a pragmatic and moderate course on this matter, at least since the Rooseveltian handling of the Mexican expropriation of oil companies in 1934, a case in which the claims of the companies obtained only a modicum of support from the Administration, political reasons for a settlement being judged to overwhelm private interests. This tradition has been maintained with minor changes. During the 1962 discussion of the Foreign Assistance Act, however, provisions had been inserted directing the United States Administration to suspend aid in case of expropriations not followed by "appropriate steps," which may include arbitration, to provide "equitable and speedy compensation in convertible foreign exchange, as required by international law."

Such a provision, unless wisely administered, may become a source of interminable friction in U.S. relations with the Latin American countries, which are likely to question (a) the implied assumption that compensation in convertible foreign exchange is required under international law, when the legal tradition supports only the requirement that compensation be made in a *"useful"* form of payment; (b) the premature internationalization of the disputes, in view of the fact that, unless and until denial of justice by local courts is demonstrated, litigation between individual companies and sovereign states remains a matter of internal and not international law; (c) foreign-assistance programs which may be transformed into a dangerous leverage by private interests in support of exaggerated claims on foreign governments.

The Controversy on Planning

A useless and frustrating dispute on planning versus free enterprise lurked below the surface during several of the inter-American economic conferences of the postwar period.

Various Latin American countries—desirous of assuring continuity of financing arrangements, of obtaining global financial commitments on a program basis rather than on a project-by-project basis, and of expanding themselves as an instrument for mobilization of popular support for economic development—pressed for recognition of the principle of planning and programming and for the acceptance, by the United States, both in its own financial agencies and through its representatives in international organizations, of long-term financial commitments.

The idea of long-range planning and programming found reluctant ears among United States policy-makers who were preoccupied with avoiding a massive United States involvement in financial commitments for aid to Latin America, and fearful that the endorsement of the planning philosophy might encourage or hasten state-minded or socialist tendencies in Latin American governments, thus stifling private enterprise.

The United States attitudes began to show perceptible changes after the launching of Operation Pan America, and particularly during the discussion of the Committee of Nine and Bogota Conference in June and September of 1960, respectively. Only in the Punta del Este Charter, however, was there a frank and strong endorsement of the principle of long-range global planning and the correlate acceptance of a long-run United States commitment for Latin American development.

As usual, this shift in policy has not been devoid of paradoxes. For after having insisted over many years on United States' acceptance of the planning philosophy, many Latin American countries found themselves administratively and technically unequipped for undertaking the planning job when the principle was finally recognized at Punta del Este. Substantial progress is being made in this direction, and one of the major tasks of technical assistance in the near future will be the improvement of the planning machinery on this continent.

The Alliance for Progress

By far the most important event in recent days in inter-American relations is the launching of the Alliance for Progress.

The Alliance for Progress was built on the foundation laid down by the proposal of the Operation Pan America made by Brazilian President Kubitschek. It has with the latter points of contact and points of dissimilarity. They both aim at quantifying growth objectives for Latin American countries, at determining needed rates of investment and the magnitude and sources of the required external assistance, and both recognize the collective responsibility of the Americas in the fight against economic underdevelopment. They differ in that the Alliance for Progress lays emphasis on the immediate promotion of social investment and on long-run institutional and structural reforms, which were not focused upon by Operation Pan America. The latter envisaged social development as a by-product of economic development and held that the effectuation of reforms should be a result rather than a pre-condition of the global investment effort.

The simple enunciation of the Alliance for Progress has brought a significant short-run reduction of tensions in the Hemisphere. Many of its postulates give recognition to long-standing claims of enlightened Latin American statesmen and economists. Whether or not its final result will be a permanent abatement of tensions depends obviously on methods, pace, and success of implementation.

As is inevitable in programs of social transformation, internal tensions are generated during and within the very process of change. If a taxonomy of tensions were attempted one might distinguish between the *transformative* tensions and the *operational* tensions. The first are unavoidable and necessary for they are at the very core of the problem of changing social aims, attitudes, and values. The process of modernization of societies is never a spontaneous process, but is always a promoted change, in which the elements of the old social order are subject to transformation or destruction. The "operational" tensions are those generated by imperfections and strain in the machinery for implementation of a complex program of social change and economic development, operated on an international scale. In a sense, the *transformation* tensions refer to *terminal* values and the *operational* ones to *instrumental* values.

I have, in a different context, sought to analyse the unresolved "antinomies" that beset the Alliance for Progress. This may provide a convenient framework to discuss both the transformative and operational tensions.

The *first antinomy* is the contrast between the instrument and the objective. The Alliance for Progress is a bold program for economic development and social change with a strong egalitarian bent. But some of the governments that signed the Punta del Este Charter, fortunately a very small minority, still represent traditional rural oligarchies whose allegiance to drastic social change is either too superficial or too timid. In such cases the implementation of social reforms will be impelled much less by the carrot of social justice and economic development than by the stick of fear of social convulsion.

The *second* is the contradiction between the need for an impact effect and the conditions of maximum long-run effectiveness. The latter require an adequate institutional framework, structural reforms of tax and land-tenure systems, and a coherent set of monetary and fiscal policies, in order to allow the investments to attain an optimum yield and to assure a proper coefficient of self-help.

On the other hand, it is often necessary, for social and political reasons, to direct immediately some initial investment to several sectors of the underdeveloped economy even before social reforms are enacted and effective economic policies adopted. A certain risk of initial waste must therefore be accepted, almost, we might say, as the political cost of breaking inertia and arousing public support and participation; and there is no way of avoiding a partial misallocation of resources, except at the much higher cost of generating skepticism and mistrust regarding the purposes and effectiveness of the Alliance.

Third, we have the controversy between social and economic development. The Alliance has been sometimes criticized, particularly in Brazil, as a method of dealing with social problems by means of social remedies, while those problems require, to a great extent, basically economic solutions. Yet, when the prevailing social environment is such that the available labor force cannot be fully engaged in production on account of social unrest, squalor, and disease, then it is sensible to complement massive economic investments with allocations of capital for social development projects. In fact, economic and social investments instead of being mutually exclusive alternatives become indeed complementary.

Fourth, we face the serious dilemma of consented reform versus revolutionary change. One could easily draw the *divortium aquarum* of contemporary social action and thought in Latin America as coinciding with the line that divides the will to bring about basic economic, social, and political reforms (even of a radical nature) by means of democratic change, from the desire to subvert existing institutions, in order to impose upon social reality, in a sudden manner, new patterns and values. Here we find both the extremes of left and right, the revolutionaries and the defenders of the status quo, fighting in the same trench, although for opposite reasons, against the Alliance for Progress. The former because they do not want to work toward gradual progress, but rather try to extract light from darkness, and economic order from social chaos. The latter because they do not want to lose the comfortable status they have enjoyed for so many years in our unjustly organized societies, afflicted by the contrast between despair and privilege.

In the *fifth place,* there is the dilemma between government planning and free enterprise. Social pressures for development in the modern context require a large degree of government intervention, which, if not skillfully handled, may have restraining effects on the vigor of private initiative. Moreover, political factors may impose the reservation on special areas for national operation. It is far from easy to maintain a correct balance between private motivation and planned growth, and it may be expected that tensions will arise between governments and private enterprises, particularly foreign enterprises. The use of the leverage of external assistance to interfere with the government's freedom of choice in allocating tasks between the public and the private sector may generate dangerous friction which it is imperative to avoid if the Alliance for Progress is to succeed.

Let us register, as a *sixth factor,* the conflict between political inspiration and bureaucratic inertia. And this both in the giving and in the receiving end. The new mood, the new tempo, the new magnitude of effort finds enemies in conventional attitudes of the Washington lending agencies, for instance, that, adhering to conventional banking criteria, are always prone to reduce their own effort when new sources of funds enter the field; as well as in the incoherence of receiving countries often unable to modernize their administrative and planning machinery. In fact, bureaucratic perspiration threatens to sap the vigor of the political inspiration of the Alliance.

Finally we come to the antinomy of trade versus aid. It has been estimated that the decline in the dollar receipts of Latin American countries, as a result of declining prices of their exports to the United States, is comparable, and in some instances in the last few years superior, to the dollars received in the form of loans and grants from the U.S. Since 1953 the weighted U.S. average price of Latin American imports (excluding Venezuela and Cuba) declined by 20 percent, while U.S. export prices rose by 10 percent. The value of exports of Latin America to the U.S. in 1961 (assuming a relatively low price elasticity of U.S. demand for those exports) could have been higher by some U.S. $1.4 billion, if prices had remained at the 1953 level, a year which may be taken as a reasonable basis for comparison because it was not distorted either by the abnormal demand of the preceding Korean boom or by the coffee valorization prices of 1954. This sum is superior to the combined flow of funds from all sources into Latin America last year. This perhaps provides a clue to the frustrating fact that despite a substantial flow of funds to Latin America in the last decade, the perilous drift toward stagnation or abatement of growth in the countries south of the Rio Grande has not been slowed.

It is true that the price decline is a market phenomenon and not the result of an international conspiracy, and that to a certain extent the Latin American countries themselves contributed to the weakening of their terms of trade, through unrealistic production and trade policies. The problem, however, is not to allocate guilt but merely to verify objectively that in a net sense there has not been a transfer of real resources to Latin America and that neither the U.S. nor the industrialized countries of Western Europe (which unlike the United States have benefited from improved terms of trade without an off-setting lending effort) have lost treasure or substance in helping Latin America. It should be noted that while both the American taxpayers and Congress acted generously in accepting the burden of taxes for foreign aid, there is sometimes a tendency to forget the savings which the American consumer realized through lower prices paid for imports from Latin America; or to exaggerate the financial effort imposed by the Alliance for Progress, which not only represents, at currently estimated amounts, less than one-fourth of the yearly outlays for the Marshall Plan, and which comes at a time when the American economy does not suffer inflationary pressure but, on the contrary, has substantial idle industrial capacity, food surpluses, and unemployed human resources.

The solution of these unresolved antinomies will be of fateful import for the Alliance for Progress. They affect and involve both North Americans and Latin Americans. For anguishing contradictions and conflicting motivations are not a privilege of either side, but part of the human burden, that can only be conquered by united effort. But more is required. There are political and psychological preconditions. Among them the most important is the creation of a mystique (I prefer to talk of *mystique* rather than of *ideology* because the latter word has been often tainted by the evil scent of regimentation and intolerance).

For the Alliance is not an exercise in a political vacuum. It is a work of social engineering requiring from the people a passionate involvement. In this sense it has to act as counter-myth to the Communist ideology which, despite its wanton brutality, has been rather successful in conveying to neglected masses a feeling of belonging in the construction of new societies. For the program of the Alliance to succeed, men's minds and hearts must be mobilized, old traditions crushed, privileges waived, social injustices corrected.

The problem is to instill in the masses in Latin America a sense of *personal* as well as of *national* commitment. This personal involvement would require, at the outset, the breaking of inertia and skepticism. In other words, we must improve the credibility of the Alliance. That is why actual deeds in the form of well chosen impact projects to reach the masses are needed immediately, independent of social and structural reform, and independent of prior satisfaction (by governments often paralyzed by strife or insufficiently committed to the reformist purpose of the Alliance) of requirements of planning and financial stability.

But a sense of *national involvement* must also be created. As Governor Muñoz Marín of Puerto Rico has put it, the "ideals of the Alliance must be fused with the national ideals of each country." Those national ideals may take the form of plans, programs, or simply development strategies. What is essential is that they represent the national aspirations and not the importation of a foreign mold, for otherwise they would not provoke a national involvement in the concept of democratic reform and change.

Finally, since the Alliance is a cooperative continental undertaking, the organs for political expression and multilateral action must be strengthened just as, in the European case, a "mystique of unity" was created by a succession of associative organs, both in the economic and in the political fields—the OEEC under the auspices of the Marshall Plan, the Council of Europe, the Coal and Steel Community, the Western European Union, and above all the Common Market. Hence the suggestion, now often heard, that the creation in the inter-American scene of executive organs to promote economic integration—fashioning perhaps a "hemispheric nationalism," to use Felipe Herrera's expression—as well as of a political body, possibly in the form of a Western Hemisphere Parliament, may prove instrumental in fostering the *mystique* of the Alliance. For the politics of the Alliance are just as important as its economics.[8]

The Alliance for Progress offers what may be the last chance to reduce economic, social, and political tensions of the impatient and impoverished masses of Latin America to levels compatible with democratic reforms, without the painful and often uncontrollable surgery of authoritarian revolution. Bold faith is needed no less than patient toil. There must be a constant search for understanding, and there must be courage to make mistakes because of excessive faith, rather than stagnate through caution or conventional wisdom.

To make the Alliance succeed is the great and perilous but rewarding travail of the Americas in this fateful decade.

[8] See Felipe Herrera, president of the Inter-American Development Bank, "The Economic Aspects of the Alliance for Progress," an address at Georgetown University, Washington, D.C., June 27, 1962.

Problems of Government Policy and Administration in Latin American Development[1]

That an economist should discuss the problems of public administration is not as contradictory as it may at first seem. Of recent years the demarcations between economics and some of the other social-science disciplines have grown increasingly flexible, and economists have been finding their knowledge and their opinions of growing value to their fellow social scientists. For this broadening of influence we can find a number of reasons.

The first is that substantial conceptual modifications have been introduced recently in the study of economics, by what we call "developmental economics." This change has resulted from the great emphasis now placed on the so-called nonconventional inputs: organization, technology, management, and entrepreneurship. Until recently the emphasis of the economists was much more on the conventional factors of production, or inputs under the general headings of land, labor, and capital. Looking now more closely at the intriguing and difficult problem of development, the economists are discovering that they were guilty of a mechanicist illusion, having over-emphasized the importance of physical investment in roads, dams, buildings, and the like, and under-estimated the enormous contribution of qualitative improvements of the human factors of production, through technology, organization, management, and entrepreneurship.

The second reason why economists are now much more inclined to discuss problems in other social sciences, particularly in the complicated and unreliable art of administration and governing, is the realization of the difference between the "spontaneous" type of development, which was characteristic of most economic growth during the nine-

[1] A lecture given in the Jump-McKillop Memorial Lecture Series in Public Administration, delivered at the Graduate School of the U.S. Department of Agriculture, Washington, D.C., on November 7, 1963.

teenth century, and the present pattern of what we call "derived development."

In the first model of development, which was roughly the one according to which both the United States and Great Britain evolved, development was very vigorously pushed by the entrepreneurship of individuals or groups or families, possessed by a special demon, the need-achievement (to use a pedantic word of modern psychology). This demon found its manifestation in the competitive spirit, in the acceptance of technological change, in the propensity to innovate. In the present-day pattern of "derived development," it is the masses rather than the vigorous entrepreneur that, by applying pressure for increased consumption, impel the governments to take a leading function in promoting economic development.

This derived pattern of development leads to one important consequence. It necessitates a much greater degree of government intervention as an organizer and motivator in the growth process. Accordingly, public administration has a much more important role, and programming and planning—which are aspects of public administration—receive a much greater emphasis.

It is true, of course, that in addition to those basic problems of motivation and impulse, there are other reasons requiring public administration to play a much greater role in the present-day developing countries than was the case in the countries of earlier industrialization. Among these reasons, I would cite the following: (a) imperfection and smallness of markets leading often to dangerous private monopolies that may have to be averted or restrained by government intervention; (b) the abnormal uncertainty and risk in periods of rapid economic and social transformation, which act as a deterrent to private entrepreneurs; (c) equity considerations, that impose the need for reducing income disparities, either between persons or between regions, a task for which the fiscal system is the only adequate instrument.

Thus public administration turns out, increasingly, to be one of the first chapters of any rational theory of economic growth. While relevant for all of the developing countries, public administration in the emerging countries of Africa and Asia must undertake tasks which go far beyond directing the organizational process in economic and social fields. It has the immense task of creating a national unity and a national personality capable of surmounting the centrifugal force of tribal and regional rivalries, and, on the other hand, of instilling the ferment of change in traditional societies.

In Latin America, where countries achieved their political independence over a century ago, but still linger in the throes of underdevelopment, the task is narrower than in Africa and Asia, but no less important. That task is to organize the governmental participation in economic and social development and to launch the reforms designed for modernization of the societies.

In this discussion I shall confine myself largely to public administration in Latin America. I shall not attempt any detailed list of techniques, flaws, or possible improvements, because there are many competent public administrators who could better analyze this type of problem. Neither shall I dwell on individual malfunctions of the public administration system in Latin America. Instead, I shall concern myself largely with general economic and social questions, such as attitudes and motivations, which are both preconditions and conditioning factors of public administration. This essay will be thus more a disquisition on the economic and social background within which public administration has to operate in Latin America, than on any specific field of public administration.

THE PSYCHOSOCIAL BACKGROUND OF PUBLIC ADMINISTRATION

If we attempt to examine attitudes toward public administration in Latin America, we shall find a number of adverse psychosocial attitudes, which it is important to examine objectively. The main impediment to improvement of public administration in Latin America is perhaps the tradition of *state paternalism* that is present in practically all of the countries. There are several consequences of this traditional trait. It affects the recruitment of employees, which is more often than not conducted by the system of affiliation or allegiance to political clienteles rather than by systems designed to measure concrete achievement; it encourages padding of government offices; it tends to insulate state enterprises from the winds of competition; and it explains the generally flabby nature of the control procedures over government operations and government enterprises.

The prevalence of paternalist attitudes varies greatly from country to country and several of them have already made a dent in this tradition by developing objective systems for evaluation of performance and recruitment of personnel. By and large, however, there remains an unhealthy inheritance of paternalistic elements in the administration, which prevents that impersonal handling of public affairs, conducive to impartiality of administration and efficiency of operations.

Another traditional flaw of attitude is what I might call the *overcentralization in decision-making*. This may manifest itself both at the regional level and at the sectoral level. At the regional level, there is an excessive weakness of provincial and local governments, leading to overconcentration of decision-making at the center. In fact, I recall that one of the most plausible rationalizations advanced in favor of the construction of Brasilia, the new capital of Brazil, was that it might be the only way of preventing the President of the Republic from continuing to be in effect, though not in name, the mayor of Rio de Janeiro, compelled to take cognizance of minute problems of city administration.

At the sectoral level there is clear evidence of this same basic flaw in attitude. There is relatively little room for delegation of authority both because of the low level of competence in intermediate echelons of the public service and because of the reluctance of the middle layers to take on or accept responsibility for policy decisions. This has led to a peculiarly perverse solution which in fact does not solve the problem at all. It is the excessive fragmentation of the administrative machinery by the creation of autonomous agencies, which do manage to *decentralize* somewhat the decision-making process but at the cost of ruining the mechanism for centralized control, for evaluation of performance, and for establishment of working norms. Thus, more flexibility in decision-making is attained only by impairing the mechanism for administrative coordination.

Needed: A Theory of Governmental Intervention

A third problem which is vital in the analysis of the present public administration picture in Latin America is the *absence of an adequate and realistic theory on the role and limits of government intervention*. Throughout the continent one finds complete lack of faith in regulatory powers of the government, paralleled by an overconfidence in the managerial performance of government enterprises as well as an underestimation of the waste involved in the excessive and premature socialization of many enterprises.

Several distortions arise from the lack of a proper theory on the limits and role of government intervention. One is the continuous temptation of government organizations and enterprises to indulge in what we might call "subsidy pricing," namely, the charging for services at rates that are inadequate to cover the costs or to finance expansion. This

Government Policy and Administration

leads to a wrong distribution of the financial burden of state services, which are transferred from the user to the general public through inflationary deficits or through general taxation, when specific taxation or levying of adequate user charges for the cost of services would be the correct solution. There is also the problem of politicization of management, which is an almost inevitable consequence of often ill-concealed attempts to enlarge the area of government intervention, prompted by the lack of faith in the efficacy of government regulatory powers. Let us mention finally the old problem of absence or inadequacy of sanction against inefficiency and corruption in government enterprises.

There is scarcely, therefore, an area in which deep thought and correct formulation is more needed than in the devising of a theory to direct governmental intervention, in countries at our stage and level of development.

Two premises must be recognized at the outset. The first is that in the underdeveloped countries of Latin America, as well as in other developing countries, a much greater degree of government intervention is needed and desirable than is the case in mature, cumulative-growth economies, such as, for instance, that of the United States. This need for greater government intervention exists even though, admittedly, the level of governmental efficiency tends to be much lower. The reasons behind this need are not only the fact that traditional areas of investment—such as social overhead outlays for health and education as well as economic overhead outlays for flood control, irrigation, sanitation, or road-building—are of overwhelming importance in the early stage of development, but that even in the directly productive sectors there is need for special incentive and government action. A few cases can be cited to justify government intervention beyond the traditional area of investment.

First, the need for *pioneer investment* in the opening of new areas and in creating sources of power. Another motivation, which is somewhat more debatable but still important, is what might be called *preclusive investment* arising from the need to implant government monopolies as a deliberate measure to prevent the creation of private monopolies. There is, thirdly, the need for *suppletory investment* in cases where the technical lumpiness of the investment or technological progress necessitate changing the scale of investment. In Brazil, for instance, government intervention was proven necessary (and this was the case also in Argentina) when the problem was to change the scale of steel production from small charcoal furnaces to modern open-hearth steel-making procedures, requiring a substantial accumulation of capital that lay beyond the capabilities of private enterprise at the present level of private savings and investment. There is, finally, what we might call *expiatory investment*, which is an attempt of the government to correct bottlenecks in several investment sectors—such as power and transportation—resulting in many cases from inadequate incentives or punitive policies in relation to private enterprise. This has been the case in practically all Latin America, where privately owned railways, and in some cases, electric power companies, proved incapable of financing their upkeep and expansion in the face of rigid tariff rates in an age of inflation. The government had then to intervene to expiate the original punishment visited on private enterprise and to undertake a job of its own. To these reasons I might add the need for assuring a better *distribution of investment and income* between regions.

There are thus several powerful reasons why the scale, intensity, and frequency of government intervention in Latin American economies is bound to be much greater than that which would be considered advisable or rational in some other countries. But there is a second important premise, which is often overlooked in Latin America. That is that the only criterion for the division of roles as between public and private enterprise should be their respective suitability and efficiency for the assigned tasks. I am using the term suitability in a broad fashion to cover also political and security considerations of a paramount nature that make necessary or advisable the presence of the government. This second basic premise is often overlooked in Latin America where the debate between private enterprise and governmental intervention is based on ideological lines rather than on a pragmatical evaluation of the relative efficiencies of the two sectors in fulfilling any specific task.

I would like to expatiate on those two premises in an attempt to develop some policy norms that might throw light on this emotionally debated problem of government versus private enterprise in Latin America.

The *first* norm would be that whenever feasible indirect controls through credit, taxation, and foreign-exchange policies should be preferred to direct controls and to administrative rationing, basically for two reasons: the technical and ethical problems inherent to the administration of direct controls; and the desirability of preserving some of the

Government Policy and Administration

basic allocating and guiding functions of the price system. The *second* norm would be that regulatory controls should be in principle preferred to direct managerial control, and the latter to full ownership by the government. This principle is based again on two considerations: the fact that the government's financial and managerial resources are inadequate in Latin America even for those traditional tasks which are completely inaccessible to private enterprise; the fact that the socially desirable controls can in most cases—though not in all, of course—be enforced without either managerial control or full ownership by the government. The *third* norm would be that government investment as a rule should concentrate on the economic and social overhead, exceptions being made, however, to admit and encourage government intervention even in directly productive sectors, when the following conditions prevail: (a) when there is "capital lumpiness," that is when the size of the investment effort is so capital-intensive that it exceeds the capability of private enterprise to mobilize resources; (b) when there is need for pioneering either in a regional sense—the opening of new regions—or in a technological sense—the implantation of new techniques; (c) when the maturation period exceeds the waiting capacity of private enterpreneurs; this often turns out to be the case in modern technology when the construction of large steel mills or large dams require four or five years, so that economic profitability is not reached until an exaggerated period elapses, a period which exceeds the saving capacity of private enterprise; and (d) when there is need for avoiding the formation of private monopolies which may become sources of excessive private power or private exploitation. A *fourth* norm would be that government operational intervention, when needed, should take the form of mixed companies with private participation in financing, management, and control, rather than the form of state monopolies, except when security or strategic considerations are paramount. A *fifth* norm would be that government planning and investment should be based on noninflationary methods of raising resources through taxation, internal borrowing, or foreign loans, rather than on deficit financing, although the latter may be resorted to on a limited scale. Perhaps one could add *another norm* that experience has proven extremely difficult to implement, which is that the government should preserve its capacity and willingness to withdraw from a sector after the pioneering stage is completed. I say advisedly that this is a difficult norm to follow because having been a development banker, in charge of promoting government investment in several fields, I found it practically impossible to withdraw state participation from a project even after the child had well surmounted the weaning stage.

I expatiated a bit on the scope, limits, and rationale of government intervention because I believe it is at the very core of the problem of public administration in Latin America, where a comparatively small number of skilled administrators are saddled with quite impossible tasks; for not only do they have to conduct the normal operations of the government, but also to supervise a proliferation of government enterprises and entities, in fields that could best be handled by simple regulatory controls, if only our statesmen were less skeptical about the effectiveness of regulatory controls and more skeptical about the efficacy of government management.

It seems to be a peculiar twist of opinion that many people, while recognizing that a regulatory agency requires a smaller number of trained personnel, and therefore could be more adequately staffed than a whole host of different government agencies, still prefer somehow to face the awesome responsibility of direct administration instead of relying on a relatively small and effective body of regulators.

The Problem of Discontinuity

Let me now deal with another problem of public administration in Latin America which I would call "abnormal discontinuity." Discontinuity in administration takes place both at the operational level and at the policy-making level. At the operational level, the frequent succession of governments produces a civil service that is floating without real roots—which does not benefit from regulated recruitment procedures and at times has no *esprit de corps*. This leads to excessive instability of the government machinery in response to changes of government. Of course, public administration is essentially a political task and the administrator cannot and should not be unresponsive to political changes. But there is some intermediate point between complete inertia, creating a divorce between political orientation and administrative behavior, and complete upheaval, with each change of administration resulting, of course, in complete disruption of the effectiveness of government operations. Fortunately, I think, substantial progress has been made in most of the Latin American countries toward endowing the civil service with a greater degree of continuity. Certainly in Brazil we have overcome a substantial part of the problem and perhaps indulged

Government Policy and Administration 53

in the opposite excess by giving excessive stability to public officials, in the effort to overcome the problem of periodical disintegration of the government machinery at the occasion of government changes.

Discontinuity at the decision-making level is what an American economist recently called "the pseudo-creative response." Each new administrator, each new government becomes sometimes possessed of a convenient amnesia and forgets all of the progress made, the research and experience accumulated, by the preceding governments. With unnecessary originality, it is decided that a fresh start must be made. This occurs only too often in our countries, although I might say that even in some much more stable and mature societies, such as the United States, one often finds succeeding governments embarking feverishly in unnecessary originality.

We might come now to what Professor Hirschman of Columbia University called the "dilemma of motivation versus understanding." In developed societies which have completed their process of maturation, technical creativeness and continuous adaptation lead to incrementalist attitudes in problem-solving. Such societies usually tackle problems when they are ready for solution and when the solution is feasible. The so-called "latecomer societies," particularly those affected by the revolution of rising expectations, on the other hand, are in a hurry to develop, and are often impatient in problem-solving. I find myself in great difficulty, I might add, to select appropriate terminology to describe the underdeveloped countries. Having been for most of the postwar period engaged in one way or the other in studies and debates on economic development, I found that the terminology develops much faster than the developing countries themselves. Originally they were called the poor countries, reflecting the rather fatalistic notion of the prewar days. Then a dynamic concept was injected—they were called the backward countries presumably because at some point they might be able to move forward. Then they were called, successively, the undeveloped countries, the underdeveloped countries, the emerging countries. Now that they are shaken by the wind of rising expectations some facetious soul has called them the "expectant countries." Well, one of the characteristics of the "expectant countries" is the attack simultaneously on many-sided problems which do not offer a real possibility of solution. Once failure results, these countries move to the other extreme and lapse into some sort of ideological fundamentalism, which is the attempt to seek a solution not by increments of reform but by drastic revolution. This basic dilemma between motivation and understanding is a serious one and undoubtedly affects the direction, meaningfulness, and effectiveness of popular decision in Latin America.

Even the conception of the Alliance for Progress is predicated on the notion that many-sided and multifarious reforms should be attempted for the modernization of society. But this poses immediately the problem of compatibility between short-run and long-run objectives that make up the grand design of the Alliance, namely agrarian reform, fiscal reform, educational reform, creation of a suitable climate for profit investment, and reasonable price stabilization. In the short run, however, it is quite questionable that those objectives are reconcilable. So while there is nothing wrong in the globalist approach, the Alliance for Progress, as a catalog of evils to be cured and as an indication of desirable reforms is apt to create more problems than it solves if this *globalist strategy* is not implemented through *incrementalist tactics*. One ought to be satisfied at times with partial incremental reforms, rather than to be overambitious and expect complete social transformation in one fell swoop.

Some of those dilemmas are already being felt in Latin America. If, for instance, one presses violently for agrarian and tax reforms, aiming at redistribution of income, it is unrealistic not to expect, at the same time, a deteriorating of the climate for private investment; after all, private investors are precisely the property groups that are likely to get panicky at the reforms. So if one ascribes priority to reform—and that is probably a correct and desirable posture—then one ought not to be too sanguine in expecting an improvement of the private-investment climate. In fact, one should be sophisticated enough to countenance its temporary deterioration. I think the North American executive is probably conscious of the existence of this problem, but from speeches that I hear in certain quarters of Congress, I note very little if any awareness there of the probability that there may be a short-run incompatibility between otherwise desirable objectives. One should not get impatient, discouraged, or otherwise irritated by the fact that, parallel with the push for reform, one has to sacrifice temporarily some other important objectives. Similarly, price-stabilization measures are desirable in themselves and useful for long-run development, but at times are rendered more difficult by the push for social equity and social justice. When the preaching of the gospel of social justice really takes hold, it is bound to stimulate claims for welfare benefits and wage revindication which, though desirable in themselves, and perhaps non-postponable, may render the achievement of price stabilization an even more complicated task than it normally is.

I think I have outlined some of the main psychosocial problems that form the context within which the public administrator has to operate in Latin America. It is my hope that some limited usefulness will be derived from this analysis, which admittedly does not go into any detailed description of Latin American administrative procedures and problems. As an economist, I would like to conclude these short notes with a quotation from the economist Kenneth Boulding, who has been pleading all along for a balanced approach to this problem of relationship between private enterprise and public administration. His way of formulating the problem brings perhaps a nice cautionary note on the way to approach these problems in Latin America. "The socialist," he says, "is likely to be too optimistic about the power of government to do good and the liberal too optimistic about the power of the market to prevent evil."

Facts and Fantasy in Brazilian Development[1]

A brief examination of the present outlook for Brazilian development can perhaps best be carried out by surveying three of the major problems facing the country's planners, and then summarizing the direction which efforts to solve these problems must take.

THE SPURIOUS OPTIONS

Among the perplexing problems confronting national planners, not by any means the least are two serious spurious options, two alternatives which in fact do not exist but which nevertheless spread poison and instill passion. The first one is the injurious and fictitious distinction between "nationalists" and "entreguistas" or "cosmopolitans." It is about time to end this sham of "abusive personalism," to use Jeremy Bentham's expression from his "Treaty of Political Sophisms." Brazil has nothing to hand over and much to discover.

In fact, many of those criticized in the past for being "sell-outers" always practiced a vigorous nationalism. In this group of defendants one may find scientists and geologists who enlarged the mineral wealth of the country and made it less dependent on the external world. Also included in this group are economists, planners, and administrators who discovered processes, formulated theories, and created efficient institutions of development.

If the word is freed from its totalitarian and demagogic distortions, we must all be *nationalists*. The option is spurious. Aside from the Communist minority which is denationalizing by doctrine, the valid distinction I see on the basis of my analysis of men and things is between *pragmatic* or functional nationalists and *romantic* or temperamental nationalists. The latter confuse intentions with results. They

[1] An address given in Rio de Janeiro on the occasion of the nomination of Roberto Campos for the *Visão* magazine award as "Man of the Year," in August, 1961.

start with enthusiasm and end in fanaticism, this being, according to Santayana, "the art of redoubling efforts after losing sight of objectives." Often they espouse an inconsistent theory of development, wishing at the same time more consumption, more investment, and less capital inflow. They want more investment from the government and more social benefits, and, at the same time, lower taxes. They want the national entrepreneur strengthened, but mutilate him with disturbing interventions by the state and incompetent manipulation of the price system. They want the results of development, but not the means to achieve it. Many of them, though they do not confess it, favor the dangerous surgery of revolution.

The pragmatic nationalist seeks to operate within the frame of democratic institutions and prefers reform to revolution. As to myself, I shall continue considering myself a pragmatic nationalist. I renounce the temptation of mobilizing resentment in order to gain the authority to plan development. I would rather strengthen the national entrepreneur than merely antagonize the foreigner. I would want the state not to do what it cannot do, in order to do what it should do. I prefer to love my own country rather than to hate the others.

The second spurious option is between stabilization and development. Inflation, like all fevers, has a stimulating phase; but like all fevers, it corrodes the organism. The spurious option is no option. We should pursue development in a context of stability, because only in this way shall we transform a passing excitement into a safe journey.

The Illusions of Development

A realistic approach to the problem of economic development presupposes the capacity to overcome illusions. One of the most prevalent of these, at the moment, is the *"transpositional illusion."* This is the idea that resources are magically multiplied and costs reduced by the mere change of the economic agent—from private enterprise to the state. The reluctance of the people to accept the direct cost of operation of services and their endless patience in bearing the indirect and cruel taxation brought about by state deficits exemplify this illusion.

The second is the *"distributive illusion."* This illusion asserts that the raising of the standard of living of the population can be accomplished directly through regulation of capitalist "selfishness," instead of being, as it indeed is, a by-product of economic development. A delicate balance must be maintained between fiscal measures for income distribution and social benefits indispensable for the creation of an internal market large enough to justify a speedy economic growth, on the one hand, and the accumulation of public resources and private funds for investment, on the other.

The third is the *"mechanistic illusion."* This consists of an overemphasis on physical investments in machines and buildings, as compared with investment in education and technology. But the physical investment is of no value without men trained to use the buildings and to guide the machines. And all recent research on economic growth in the Western world indicates that at least half of this growth was due not to equipment and the quantity of manpower but to the improvement of productivity derived from education and technology. Another mechanistic exaggeration is the emphasis on industry, to the neglect of agriculture. This emphasis threatens the industrialization surge itself through the inflated costs of foodstuffs and the scarcity of foreign exchanges derived from a paucity of exports.

The Great Conflict

But the key problem of present-day Brazil lies, perhaps, neither in the spurious options nor in the illusions of development. It hinges rather on a sound solution of some contradictions in our development process. Among these the most important is perhaps the hidden controversy on the role of the state and the limits for its intervention. In this matter, there is no point in being dogmatic, since both extreme positions—that of the socialist and that of the liberal—are naïve.

The preoccupation with state intervention—so strong among us today—has valid roots and perverse roots. The important thing is to separate the wheat from the chaff, so that we may arrive at a social and Christian capitalism and not at a hybrid and inefficient system, which only externally keeps the appearance of a capitalistic system but is devoid of vitality and motivation.

Few today would question the need, in underdeveloped countries like Brazil, for a greater degree of state intervention than that which guided the development of the United States, Canada, and the majority of countries in Western Europe. Among the valid reasons for this fact are, first, the nature of the developmental process, originating less from the vigor of the private entrepreneur than from the claims of the masses for a better living; second, the flaws of the price system and the market mechanism, which create the need for regulatory government intervention to restrain monopolies, to preserve competition, and to decrease excessive imbalances between people and regions in the distribution of national income; third, technological factors demanding massive investments in large production units above the resource-mobilizing capacity of private enterprise; fourth, the existence of critical areas of investment relevant to national security.

But along with these valid reasons for state intervention, there are spurious motives which sap the vitality of the system and transform such intervention into a factor disheartening to private enterprise, which cause capitalism's vigor to be lost without the discipline of socialism being gained. These motivations are (a) the "subsidy mentality" which disguises the real cost of the goods or services, making impossible the direct coverage of costs, and replaces it by taxes and subsidies; (b) the "paternalist tradition," which enlarges the area of state intervention merely for the purpose of providing more jobs; (c) the "ideological bias," which leads many to support the widening of state action as a means for the surreptitious establishment of socialism.

Our society will lose its operational efficiency if a clear and stable delimitation of areas is not arrived at as early as possible, withholding for the state those areas where technical reasons exist for believing that the state activity will be more efficient, and taking advantage elsewhere of that vigor of private enterprise which permitted the capitalism of the Western vanguard to achieve a standard of living which in socialism is still a promise.

The Task of Development

What is my vision as to the crucial direction that our effort should take in the coming years, filled as those years are with danger and promise?

The first task is to mobilize for investment the hidden sources of savings. This would either make the contribution of foreign capital less necessary or permit an equal volume of external help to be turned into a higher rate of development. Unexplored sources of savings can be tapped by curbing extravagant consumption; by utilizing the idle capacity of industry—a move facilitated by the recent exchange reform; by abandoning the excessive subsidization of public services, thus avoiding the frittering away of resources for coverage of operational deficits when they could be used for investment; by concentrating on priority investments instead of scattering resources; by reducing military expenditures; by restoring monetary stability, which will make individual savings an advantage and not a spoliation.

The next task is the solution of problems arising from our insufficient capacity to export, which threatens to strangle our development. The third task is the improvement of the governmental machinery through the training of planners and administrators. The fourth task calls for a massive effort designed to raise the general level of education and technology. The fruits of such an effort will be gains in productivity that will be a generous multiple of investments.

Only by attacking with rationality and obstinacy the problems which face Brazil and the tasks which offer some solution to those problems can we make it possible for social and economic development to become a living reality and not just a "great and useless desire."

Management, Entrepreneurship, and Economic Development[1]

I have a deep respect for the work and the techniques of the industrial engineer as well as a great deal of envy. As the engineer labors to change reality for a better and more affluent world, he does not have to put down a barrier of words and prejudices of an irrational and inefficient nature in order to be able to execute the needed tasks and to tackle the objective transformations that are solely relevant for the accomplishment of the desired effects.

In the world of economists and diplomats, on the other hand, there is not much room for quick and purposeful interventions, with clearly delineated scope, into social and economic reality. The economist or diplomat must often wait with unflinching patience for a felicitous time to move; and sometimes he must formulate the obviously needed solutions in a carefully disguised style, so as to assure a reasonable chance of acceptance.

The engineer can work on the premise of the physician, that people want medicine because it is good for their health and, therefore, that the problem is to find the right medicine. The economist, in his more difficult world, must accept with resignation the premise of the psychiatrist, that the real problem is to deal with the motives of the patient, so that he may cease to reject the cure of his ailment.

I, as an economist and a diplomat, can undoubtedly offer the industrial engineer much useful information and many instructive insights. I would think, however, that it would be vastly more consequential and useful for the industrial engineer to visit with the economist, and particularly the diplomat. Perhaps he might teach them how to look at the world with clean eyes and touch it with constructive hands; how first to install the foundation, and then to assemble the engine; how to wait

[1] An address given at the International Conference of the American Institute of Industrial Engineers, in New York, on September 25, 1963.

for the engine to be fully operational, rather than destroy it half-built on the assumption of some hypothetical malfunction.

The Nonconventional Inputs

I would like to say a word on the recent evolution of developmental economics, an evolution which, to the dismay of economists, is pushing traditional economic science very much to the background. The first and most important finding, valid both for capitalist and socialist economies, is that not more than one third of the increments of growth and productivity that took place in developed societies within our range of statistical observation can be explained by the conventional inputs—equipment, land, and quantity of labor. By far the largest part of progress is traceable to almost unquantifiable improvements in the human factor: acquisition of skills, technological innovations, entrepreneurship, and managerial organization—the nonconventional inputs. Development is thus an adventure in education complemented by physical efforts and achievement, much more than it is a simple composition in bricks and metal.

Economists and engineers alike must share the blame for thinking almost exclusively in terms of physical investments. We have indeed fallen prey to "mechanicist" illusions.

The second concept involves the difference between "spontaneous" and "derived" development. The growth, during the nineteenth and early twentieth centuries, of most of the present developed societies was based on the vigorous push of entrepreneurship from private individuals or family groups, possessed by what psychologists now call the "need-achievement" drive—a drive which found expression in the competitive spirit, in the acceptance of technical change, in the propensity to innovate.

In societies of this type there is little need to worry about human motivation as a major problem in economic development. The formation of the human capital is taken for granted as a by-product and not as a prerequisite for general economic and social advance.

In the "derived" type of development some of the basic motivations for economic progress are often lacking. There is "entreprenertia" (entrepreneurial inertia) rather than entrepreneurship. The motivation for material advance is scant, and the propensity for fundamental science dormant. Religious patterns may have to be changed; social pat-

Management, Entrepreneurship, and Economic Development 63

terns based on affiliation and ascription have to give way to the need for achievement; market values must be recognized.

In these societies, which encompass a large number of the less developed countries and many lagging regions within the developing countries, the problem of motivating the economic effort is paramount. In such countries the urge for expanding production comes not from the spontaneous vigor of the active entrepreneur but from the claims of the passive masses; not from the innovating propensity of the producer but from the imitative capacity of the consumer.

These societies must set out to foster the emergence of entrepreneurs and managers as the indispensable leadership group for economic advance. The pattern of social organization may differ: the entrepreneurs and managers may be intellectual bureaucrats and planners, they may be authoritarian family heads or military leaders, or they may be recruited from the middle classes, through competitive ascent within a democratic framework. But rise they must. And they have to be sufficiently nonconformist to seek innovation and sufficiently deviant to escape the confines of conventional mores.

The problem of inadequate motivation can be solved through the creation of a development mystique that frees impulses impounded by tradition. This development mystique can be a "shock mystique" arising from war, revolutions, or challenges to survival. Or it may be an "emulative mystique" based on the achievement of planned growth objectives to narrow the gap in relation to the advanced countries. Both the shock mystique and the emulative mystique must be rendered operational by plans and projects which are the subject matter of the economist and the industrial engineer. This leads us to the problem of the organization of the economic effort and to the role of management.

The Rise of the Managerial Class

The creation of a managerial elite is an important part of the process of formation of human capital, particularly since such a large part of the development effort must be devoted to industrialization.

As pointed out by Professors Harbison and Myers, management can be looked at from three different perspectives. From one, it is an *economic resource* or a factor of production, at times more critically short than capital or material resources. Managerial resources are complementary to capital investment and their importance grows with the size of the investment, and the need for innovation and for achieving greater labor productivity. There is a critical minimum of managerial resources, just as there is a critical minimum of material and financial resources for the take-off along the development path.

From another perspective, management is a *system of authority*. In the less advanced countries, management by dictatorial or paternalistic rule based on ownership and family tradition is prevalent. As industrial development advances and as management becomes separated from family rule and ownership, management becomes a more complex social task, involving bargaining with labor and various degrees of labor participation in the determination of wages, rules, and work norms.

Finally, as noted by Professors Harbison and Myers, management can be regarded as a *class*. Initially, in the less developed countries, management is a rather closed elite recruited from family dynasties, government service, or the military establishment. But as the task of industrialization proceeds, the complexities of industrial operation lead to the specialization of a *professional* class of managers—innovation conscious and productivity conscious—subject to systematic training and generally more socially minded (though less paternalistic) in their approach to labor than the patrimonial or political managers of non-industrialized societies.

There is scarcely a greater need in the developing countries than that for a major educational effort to select and train a class of professional managers. Here, I believe, industrial engineers and economists can smoke the calumet of peace, for I think they provide the best raw material for the recruitment of the managerial class. The engineer has a strong point in his knowledge of the technical inputs needed in the industrial process; and a weak point in his frequent reluctance to recognize resource limitations and to adhere to a priority discipline. The economist tends to be more conscious of relative costs and priorities, but often loses some of the decisiveness and precision of the industrial engineer, and lacks the logistic ability for organizing industrial inputs, which is so important for maximizing the vigor of the industrialization effort.

Be that as it may, no sustained development can be achieved, even though material and financial resources may be available, without the human capital embodied in management. For management affects vitally the degree of efficiency in the combination of all other resources, the level of productivity of labor, and the pace of innovation. In a deep sense, as Sophocles said in the Greek tragedy, "the tower and the ship are of no avail without the man."

The lesson then of both the new theory and the practice of economic growth is that the most basic thing is the determination to develop certain cultural and psychological attitudes that constitute a precondition for sustained economic and social progress. Without them material inputs and financial recipes become mere appurtenances of the "mechanicist illusion." To acquire and practice an ideology of development should be the accepted calling of the industrial engineer, as well as that of the industrial manager, the innovating entrepreneur, the creative expert, the skillful laborer.

The Training of the Managerial Class

The final question which I want briefly to broach is that of the international transmissibility of the managerial motivation and expertise. An interesting idea has recently been propounded by Mr. David Rockefeller who called for the creation of a volunteer managerial task force of free enterprise to assist underdeveloped countries to build up their private initiative through better management. While this business counterpart of the Peace Corps, as some newspapers saluted it, might be of great help to our countries, we here face head on one of the several vicious circles of economic development. For while mechanical equipment and industrial techniques are importable and transmissible, managerial attitudes are part of the social, political, and institutional fabric, and cannot easily be imported without an exasperatingly long period of adaptation. In this sense, while rules of management can be formulated and transmitted, the political and social complexities of the managerial performance have to be experienced in their own habitat. Thus the training of managers *in loco* and visits of managers from the less developed countries to the more advanced societies for exchange of experience are, in the long run, the best solutions, even though the "Business Corps" idea may be useful on a limited scale (particularly for countries in a very early stage of development where a native class of entrepreneurs and managers is yet to be born).

Concluding Words

Industrial engineers, economists, entrepreneurs, and managers should join in the great quest of our time—the quest for abundance.

There is some consolation in the fact that we may be entering an era in which the technical complexities of the managerial job may increase because of cybernetics and automation, while the human complexities of the task may decrease—for the main task may become communication between men and machines rather than between man and man. As Robert Theobald recently put it, we are moving beyond the "industrial" revolution, which was based on the combination of the power of the machine with the power of the human being into the "cybernetic revolution," in which the power of the machine is combined with the skill of the machine to produce an era of abundance.

Social Engineering and Economic Development[1]

The anguished study of the principles, problems, and policies of economic development has brought economists to a humble acceptance of the interdisciplinary approach to social sciences, an approach which they resisted for a long time. The stricture of economist Kenneth Boulding that people who talk about cross-fertilization of social sciences do so only because they have nothing better to do and nothing to say in their own sciences, may prove ill founded if we ever come to understand the mechanism for growth. I am more and more convinced that the foundation of the theory of growth has much more to do with psychology, social institutions, and ethical values than with the laws of rational economic behavior.

As economists we are fond of discussing economic development in terms of relations between input and output. We lay stress on financial capital and on plant and equipment. This type of analysis, which has interpretative and operational value in the context of the developed societies, is found wanting when the problem is to discover the inner workings of the engine of growth. It is found wanting on two counts: first, the ideological and institutional conditions, taken for granted in traditional analysis of the essentially spontaneous and gradual development of Western Europe and the United States, have limited applicability to the growth process and policy issues of what we might call "derived development"—that is, the type of development in which motivations have to be generated and institutions created or reformed as a precondition for the take-off. Secondly, even in the case of the more industrialized societies more than half of the past increases in income and productivity could not be traced to the inputs of capital and labor traditionally dealt with in conventional economics. Other highly important inputs—such as education, technology, and the sense of the

[1] The Hackett Memorial Lecture delivered by Roberto Campos at the Symposium on Latin American Trade and Aid, held at The University of Texas in March, 1964.

need for economic development—turn out not to depend on the traditional economic factors at all, but on psychological and social preconditions. It seems now quite clear that behavioral attitudes are basic for the process of growth, which cannot really start and unfold unless the following prerequisites exist: (a) a minimum level of consensus so that economic development is accepted as having a valid priority for social growth, (b) a society endowed with a minimum "need-achievement," to use an expression of modern psychology, and not totally bound by ascription, (c) acceptance of innovation for economic development, which is fundamentally a strategy for change.

Let us consider for a moment a vital question of development strategy—looking at it from a somewhat broader viewpoint than that of the economist. This will lead us to discuss in turn the problem of motivation, the problem of institutional change, of the formation of the human capital, of the mobilization of internal resources, and finally of the mobilization of external resources.

By way of introduction, let us clarify what we mean by "development" in contrast with what we mean by "progress" and "growth." Development must be regarded as a process involving structural change; it differs from "growth," which does not require structural reformation but is primarily an accretion, a widening of present structures. It differs also from the idea of "progress," which is derived largely from the values reflected in the eighteenth century optimistic humanism and the concept of preestablished harmony. The notion of development hinges much more on a structural change, than on a preestablished and automatic mechanism of growth.

Let us look for a moment at the question of motivation for development. It is motivation—rather than the investment process of which the economist talks so much—that is the starting point for a strategy of development. The level of motivation can best be raised through the creation of a development mystique which induces the population to accept the sacrifices and discipline needed for development, and prepares the ground for social and institutional changes. The mystique of development is less obvious in the historical cases of spontaneous growth and development in Western Europe and in the United States, but it is not totally absent. The "manifest destiny" idea and the appeal of the conquest of the West are genuine cases of development mystiques. So is the analogy of the "spark plug" in the German developmental effort.

The development mystique may result from historical accidents, such as the humiliation of lost wars, the crisis of independence, and

Social Engineering and Economic Development   69

challenges to survival; or it may be consciously fostered by the created images of national planners and leaders. The first case would be what we might call "shock mystique"; and the second case, "emulation mystique." Through an emulation mystique, which takes the form of setting up national objectives for growth in terms of development plans and programs, the developing country may mobilize its energy to emulate industrialized countries by narrowing the gap in productivity, wealth, income, and technology, which separates it from them. Development plans may act as polarizers of aspirations or agents of discipline and coordination. They form what one might call an "exercise in social engineering." Both the shock mystique, resulting from historical accidents, and the emulation mystique, which is deliberately created as a product of social engineering, must become operational through plans and programs; but while in the former case such plans are fundamental in helping to create the motivation and providing the ideological basis for a high need-achievement level—to borrow an expression of modern psychologists—in the latter case their main role is the rationalization of economic activity. According to their political conception and techniques of implementation, the plans may be *authoritarian* (based on compulsory allocation resources), or they may be *cooperative* (based on coordinational procedures).

Aside from the problem of creating motivation or steering it constructively, the second element in a strategy of growth is the creation or improvement of the social and political instruments for development. This element has two separate aspects. One is identifying factors in the social pattern which are inimical to development. These may be religious attitudes (such as Buddhist contemplativeness), social patterns of behavior (such as the propensity for conspicuous consumption), or patterns of land ownership and tenure. The other aspect is the development of human capital as a basic instrument for development. This process involves the formation of leadership groups and the broadening of the base of human capital, or what we might call "upgrading the masses," as opposed to creating leadership groups.

The "leadership group"—military or ideological—sets the stage for development patterns of a totalitarian nature. Alternatively, the setting may take the form of professional capitalism, in which the main leadership role is fulfilled by the national entrepreneurs, with a minimum of conscious direction being provided by a development party, a development plan, or both. It may also take the form of state capitalism, in which the development party or program is guided by a democratic middle class. Finally, it may take the form of developmental socialism. I speak of "developmental socialism" to differentiate it from traditional welfare socialism, a difference concerned mainly with the timing of, and the emphasis on, redistribution of wealth and income.

The formation of the "operating mass" involves, in its turn, a complex of measures aiming at development of human resources by motivating, organizing and concentrating the popular effort. This process includes creating a climate of achievement—selling the country on itself—and developing techniques to inspire or modify people's values, motives, and spirit.

It is in the process of organizing the operating mass for development that the problem of maintaining political stability presents itself. The very process of modernization implies social reform which, while tension-reducing in the long run, may be tension-increasing in the short run. The so-called "revolution of rising expectations" raises the level of expectancy well beyond what can immediately be achieved, often leading to impatience of revolutionary dimensions. The crucial problem of political instability emerges as a major challenge to social engineering during the developmental process, particularly if one wishes to pursue that development process within the context of conscientious democratic methods.

The third element of a strategy of development is a deliberate effort to "narrow the gap." Narrowing the gap includes both narrowing the *internal gap* within the country (with the view to national integration), and narrowing the *external gap* in income and productivity between the industrialized and the underdeveloped nations. The main components of the effort to reduce the internal gaps and thus alleviate the tensions that impede national integration are tax reforms to decrease inequalities of income, educational reforms to reduce the inequalities of social opportunities, and land reform to reduce inequalities of land distribution.

Narrowing the *internal gap* so as to create integrated societies should aim at eliminating, or at least reducing, the "dualism" between the modern urban sector and the traditional rural areas. The advance of this indispensable process of national integration, without which the effort for development cannot be conscientiously pursued, presupposes fulfillment of at least three conditions: per capita income must be rising at a perceptible rate, so that people become aware of it and break resistances to changing traditional ways; some perceptible reduction

Social Engineering and Economic Development 71

must occur in personal, sectoral, and regional differences in wealth; underemployment, the most typical form of unemployment in developing economies with primitive, unorganized markets, must be reduced. The question of narrowing the *external gap* merges with the over-all problem of accelerating the rate of economic development.

The fourth and vital component then of a strategy for development is the mobilization of internal resources. There are in most underdeveloped countries, even in the poorest ones, reserves which are less than fully exploited. Such reserves could be exploited by a better utilization of surplus labor for labor-intensive capital formation; by elimination of luxury consumption, which still prevails in many countries (due largely to unnecessary inequalities of income distribution) and which goes beyond economic stimulation and slides into ostentatious consumption; by reduction of military expenditures, or at least a change in their composition, emphasizing types of military expenditures which have a dual application, such as communications, technical training, and industries having both military and civilian purposes; by elimination of subsidies for services, which in most underdeveloped countries take the form of unrealistic and subsidized transport and utility rates, encouraging consumption at the expense of investment and constituting really a form of negative taxation; and, last but not least, by improvements in tax policies and tax administration, with a view to shifting resources from consumption to public and private investment.

The fifth element of a development strategy is the mobilization of external resources to complement the national effort. This brings me by a rather devious route to the question of "trade versus aid" in economic development. It is quite clear that trade and aid are complementary rather than alternative. They are both instruments for giving underdeveloped countries access to imported goods and services needed for investment and development. But while we need both trade and aid, exaggerated emphasis has been placed on aid, while comparatively little attention has been given to providing the developing countries with access to markets in industrialized countries. The United Nations Conference on Trade and Development now convening in Geneva is an attempt on the part of the developing countries to redress this neglect.

There is no doubt that a rather substantial difference exists between developing and industrialized countries in facing the problem of aid. To start with, we really don't like the word "aid" because it generates in the donor countries a "self-righteousness complex," or what we might call a "philanthropic syndrome." The recipient countries too often regard aid as a form of "conscience money" through which the industrialized countries seek to avoid painful political decisions regarding liberalization of trade in primary products. Both these views are no doubt unjust. Aid is certainly more a matter of self-interest than a philanthropic exercise, but then it should not be regarded either as a mere form of "conscience money."

The second, more valid, stricture made by the developing countries relates to the annulment of the effects of aid, through trade policies in industrialized countries, an annulment which brings a deterioration of the trade position of the developing ones, and which may take such forms as agricultural protectionism, fiscal duties on primary products, and resistance to importing manufactures from the developing countries under the pretext of preventing "market disruption."

Many of the Latin American countries claim that "aid" is a misnomer. It gives the impression that there has been a substantial net transfer of resources. But for Latin America in the last few years aid really played the role of compensatory financing, alleviating somewhat the problems caused by the decline in export revenue. Putting it the other way around, the decline in prices of Latin American exports reduced the burden of foreign aid on the U.S. consumer. Hence the pressure that the developing countries are bringing to bear for a substantial modification of international trade policies, and hence also the exaggerated hopes that are raised by the United Nations Conference on Trade and Development.

The proposed measures aim at several objectives. First, there are sundry proposals to expand our access to industrial markets. As an intermediate goal, we advocate free entry for tropical products, on the grounds that they do not compete with domestic activities in industrialized countries, and thus do not pose major political problems. An obstacle in the way of this liberalization scheme, we must admit, is the dissension among the developing countries themselves. Some of the developing countries now enjoy the status of Associate Members of the European Economic Community, and benefit from access to those markets. Other developing countries still enjoy the much less important, but still significant, preferential treatment within the British Commonwealth. The other developing countries—and this category includes most of Latin America—while not denying the importance of help for the newly developing countries, particularly those of Africa and Asia,

Social Engineering and Economic Development

insist that this assistance should take the form of special financial cooperation from Western Europe and not the form of discrimination against nonmember developing countries.

Another intermediate measure being advocated, before the final goal of "one-way free trade" is attained, is the elimination, particularly in Western Europe, of internal duties on such products as coffee and cocoa, which are imposed for revenue and not protectionist purposes.

A third group of measures deals with the stabilization of exchange revenues. Here several approaches are possible, and perhaps several would have to be tried in combination. One of them is the "commodity approach," exemplified by the recent international coffee agreement, designed to regulate the market by import or export. Another is the compensatory-financing approach, which is not designed to correct fluctuations of individual prices, but to offset the depressing effect of a general decline in export revenues by compensatory payments to the developing countries. There are several schemes for compensatory financing: one of them is the proposed Organization of American States (OAS) Compensation Fund, which is designed to be self-regulating over the period of an export cycle. Another is the United Nations scheme based on the insurance principle. A third, the only one now in operation, is the scheme of the International Monetary Fund, which involves an arrangement for special drawing rights to help those developing countries that suffer a decline in their over-all export revenue, by reference to a "representative" period of trade. Many of the developing countries now prefer compensatory financing to other ways of dealing with the problem. They recognize, first, that compensatory financing schemes do not stabilize individual prices and, therefore, interfere less with market trends; and second, that, provided the compensatory financing funds operate automatically (subject merely to the demonstration of export revenues), such schemes tend to decrease the possibility of political friction between the developing countries and the paying agency. This type of friction undoubtedly occurs in aid measures and also tends to occur in schemes of compensatory financing that are not automatic—such as the program of the International Monetary Fund, which involves exercise of judgment by the IMF on the cause of the decline in export revenue and on the degree of cooperation which the country concerned is giving to the IMF. The third argument for compensatory financing is that it may prove to be politically more palatable than the drastic revision in trade policies which otherwise would be necessary to achieve the goal of increasing resources for the developing countries.

A third set of measures deals with the action by developing countries themselves to diversify their exports, to launch national programs for import substitution, and to create regional markets. A recent example of a regional market is the Latin American Free Trade Association, which was preceded by the Central American Common Market. Most such programs have similar objectives, namely, to escape the confines of narrow domestic markets and to enhance their bargaining position vis-à-vis the outside world on trade-and-aid matters. A substantial increase in the flow of international resources must be a part of any development strategy of the developing countries as well as of industrialized ones. This requires mutual complementation of trade and aid and not simple substitution or mutual annulment.

Undoubtedly there are some merits in the argument often advanced by industrialized countries, especially Germany, that the managerial assistance available through aid can provide a greater stimulus than trade liberalization. It can link development assistance to local effort and self-help, and encourage the re-allocation of resources to economic development and diversification. These advantages can be, however, easily exaggerated and, in practice, have been exaggerated. They may even become negative to the extent that dispensation of aid, particularly through bilateral channels, generates political friction and tends to divert the attention of industrialized countries from the more painful trade adjustments without which the good purpose of aid can easily be nullified, as it was in the late 50's and early 60's, by the vagaries of international trade.

The enumeration of these various components of a development strategy testifies both to the complexity of the problem and to the relative impotence of economists. They know the formula for organizing economic effort but have yet to master the secrets of other social sciences—the mysterious ways of influencing psychological motivation, social behavior, and political purposes. We conclude, therefore, with a plea for cross-fertilization of the social sciences and for mutual cooperation among social scientists in tackling this anguishing problem. Let us abolish the traditional rivalries among the sociologist, the economist, and the anthropologist, each of whom thinks that the others may be brilliant but certainly not relevant.

Much greater than the challenges of physical engineering in our days is the challenge of social engineering. For unless we reduce the gap between the wealthy and the poor countries, there will be no rest and no peace in a bitter and divided world. Looming beyond the East-West conflict, and potentially much greater, is the conflict between the North and the South, between the nations that know the blessings of wealth and those whose only nourishment is hope, and whose daily companion is the bitterness of unfulfilled dreams.

Trade Opportunities of the Underdeveloped Countries[1]

Without attempting to condone the shortcomings of Brazil and perhaps of other Latin American countries in the matter of adequate policies to stimulate exports, I would like to stress the fact that these countries are encountering difficulties—both of a general nature and more specifically with regard to coffee—as a result of the trade policies pursued by the industrialized nations, traditionally importers of commodities. Among the obstacles of a general nature we might mention the changes which are occurring in the pattern of trade in primary commodities. Thus, the industrialized countries are encroaching more and more upon the area of commodity exports and are taking over markets that heretofore have belonged to nonindustrialized countries. This phenomenon does not affect directly the export revenues resulting from coffee, which is a tropical product. But the countries that depend on exports of tropical products tend to decrease their exports of competitive products, due in part to the aggressiveness of the trade policies of industrialized countries.

We see thus that between 1953 and 1960 over-all exports of primary commodities increased by 34 percent. In that period, however, commodity exports by industrialized countries grew by 57 percent, while those of nonindustrialized countries increased only by 14 percent. As a result, the nonindustrialized countries, which had 55 percent of world exports of commodities in 1953, showed a participation of 47 percent by the end of the period, while the industrialized countries had raised theirs from 45 to 53 percent. Since the nonindustrialized countries have no ready alternative for their exports, the obvious result is a decrease in their foreign-trade possibilities.

This extraordinary increase in the participation by industrialized countries in exports of primary commodities reflects in part the impact

[1] An address given during the Panel Discussion at the National Press Building, Washington, D.C., on the Pan American Coffee Day, April 17, 1963.

of American sales of agricultural surplus products, which are, within certain limits, beneficial to the underdeveloped countries, and in part the agricultural policy of the member nations of the European Common Market, on which I shall comment later in this address.

THE DETERIORATION OF THE TERMS OF TRADE

Another significant aspect of the trade in commodities is the deterioration of commodity prices. Not only is foreign trade diminishing—because the industrialized countries are taking over some of the markets of nonindustrialized countries—but a deterioration has been occurring in the prices of commodities in general and of coffee in particular, while the prices of industrial products grow higher.

We find, thus, that the over-all commodity price index fell from 100 to 93 in the period 1953–1960. This index includes petroleum, which leads to an underestimation of the margin of depreciation. If we take, for instance, products like coffee, tea, and cocoa, which are the pre-eminent tropical products, we shall find that the fall in prices was 24 percent. If we consider Brazilian coffee alone, we shall find that its index fell from 100 to 63 in 1960 and even more thereafter: a reduction of about 40 percent.

These data on price deterioration become even more significant when compared with the index of growth in the volume of trade. Thus, between 1953 and 1960 there occurred an increase of 50 percent in the volume of world trade and a deterioration of 7 percent in commodity prices. In that period, the volume of Brazilian trade grew by 20 percent and prices deteriorated by 37 percent.

FOREIGN AID AND THE FALL IN EXPORT PRICES

We can evaluate the problem in an undeniably simplified but indicative way, if we take the year 1953 as a basis and compare the revenue from coffee exports in subsequent years with that which would be obtained if that year's average export value per bag had been maintained.

Prices prevailing in 1953 are particularly suitable as a basis since they preceded the abnormal and artificial peak reached in 1954 and correspond roughly to the level of 1955 and the years immediately following. Indeed, in Brazil's case, 1955–1958 prices remained at the 1953 level. The average value per bag exported, as used in our evaluation, contains if anything a downward bias. Even on this basis, the loss will be found to be a substantial one.

It will be seen that the cumulative potential revenues foregone by Brazil amount to $2.6 billion. From 1959 on they represent some $500 million annually, an amount that would have enabled the country amply to solve all its balance-of-payment problems and increase substantially the rate of imports of goods indispensable to the process of economic development. If, in order to avoid statistical distortion, we deduct from this total the 1954 potential excess margin ($184.6 million), the total loss would still have amounted to $2.4 billion.

Merely as an example of the economic significance of this fall in revenue, let us compare these deficits in foreign currency earnings with the total United States economic aid to Brazil and to other Latin American coffee producers during the same period, including all forms of official aid of a nonmilitary nature.

The Latin American coffee-producing countries received in the period a gross sum of $3,970.5 billion in U.S. economic aid, mostly in the form of loans. Of this, $1.6 billion was allocated to Brazil, $0.65 billion to Colombia, and $1.75 billion to the other coffee producers. Now, as we have seen, Brazil alone lost, as a consequence of the fall in coffee prices, a potential revenue of between $2.4 and $2.6 billion, according to whether or not the excess of revenue in 1954 is deducted.

The purpose of these remarks is not to imply that those unfavorable trade and price movements are the result of any conscious and willful exploitative bent on the part of the industrialized coffee-consuming nations. Nor would it be fair to deny that by adopting policies leading to overproduction the primary producers visited on themselves the chastisement of price declines.

The sole purport of this arithmetical exercise on trade and aid is to provoke thought and perhaps to cast doubt on the validity and reasonableness of current complaints, now loudly heard in the U.S., about the burden of foreign aid to the taxpayer. For during the early part of the 1950's the United States consumer and taxpayer was paying much higher prices for coffee, cocoa, bananas, and other primary products from Latin America, and yet the American economy was suffering no hardship. In fact, unemployment was lower and the rate of economic growth higher than it is today, when tax-reduction is being advocated to stimulate the utilization of vast idle resources. Similarly, the Latin American economies were enjoying, on the average, a period of unprecedented growth, without any burdensome dependence on foreign aid, while now most of them are relapsing into stagnation. If, then, the

Trade Opportunities of the Underdeveloped Countries

American economy of the early 50's, with a per capita income level some 20 percent lower than it is today, was able without any visible hardship to pay, as an importer of Latin American products, sums which are appreciably greater than those currently being dispensed as foreign aid, it is difficult to escape the conclusion that the usual strictures on the alleged billions in foreign aid wastefully poured into Latin America, and on the heavy economic burden resulting therefrom, are more in the nature of political stereotypes than of sober analysis and compassionate understanding.

Restrictions on Latin American Coffee Exports

The countries of Latin America export to the countries of the European Economic Community 20 percent of their total exports and buy from the countries of the Community a comparable percentage of their imports.

But more important than the volume is the structure of this trade. Of the total Latin American exports to the E.E.C., one fifth represents coffee exports. This means that the capacity of Latin America to import equipment from the E.E.C. is conditioned to a good extent by the capacity of the latter to import coffee. Now, the member countries of the Common Market already impose, individually, heavy restrictions on coffee imports in general and, in some cases, on Latin American coffee in particular. The institution of a common external tariff will aggravate the problem by generalizing a discrimination which for the time being is not collective.

At the moment, the system of import quotas practiced by France gives a preference to imports originating in Africa and allows access by the remaining exporters to only 25 percent of annual imports into that country. Fiscal burdens imposed by the three main consumers raise the retail price to more than twice the unit value of the product at the port of arrival. In Germany, for instance, the fiscal revenues from taxes on coffee reach the astounding figure of $200 million yearly!

Evidently, elimination of these preferential taxes could lead to a considerable increase in Latin American coffee exports to the countries of the E.E.C. and, consequently, in Latin American imports from those countries. Such an evolution would be a decisive factor in the improvement of Latin American economic and financial relations with Europe, in line with the object of the concern which has been frequently shown by the United States government in associating the industrialized nations of Europe with measures of international cooperation aiming at the economic development of Latin America.

The Organization of American States has figured that Latin American coffee exports to the countries of the E.E.C. could be increased by some $130 million yearly simply through the elimination of present barriers. With the elevation of living standards in the countries of the E.E.C.—in some countries the per capita level of coffee consumption is still relatively low—the value of the additional exports could increase greatly. If we apply the level of consumption of Germany to other countries of the E.E.C., we can hope for a rise, toward the end of the decade, of some $600 million yearly in Latin American coffee exports to the E.E.C.

In this respect, it may be useful to recall the principles approved at the meeting of Ministers of Economics and Finance, held in Geneva in 1960, under the sponsorship of GATT. This document recommended especially to the contracting parties the rapid removal of quantitative restrictions which affected exports originating in underdeveloped countries; the elimination of tariffs affecting primary products exported by underdeveloped countries; the elimination or major reduction of fiscal surcharges affecting primary products exported by underdeveloped countries; the adoption by the countries having centrally planned economies of measures aiming at expansion of consumption of the aforementioned primary products; the operation of preferences in such a way as not to harm suppliers excluded from the preferential system; the limitation of subsidies paid for exports or imports of primary products; the orderly disposal of agricultural surpluses so as not to affect exports from underdeveloped countries. It remains to be seen if these recommendations will be nothing more than a pious hope or if they will find practical application.

The United States—it is but fair to say—stands out in the industrialized world as the country which, despite occasional policy contradictions, is giving of late honest recognition to the vital importance of widening trade opportunities for the developing countries. Evidence of this new attitude is the leading role played by the United States in promoting the World Coffee Agreement; in sponsoring proposals for free trade in tropical products; and in the establishment, within the IMF, of a scheme for compensatory financing to offset declines in export revenues of primary producers—although the latter scheme fails to satisfy the requirements of automaticity in the disbursement of funds, and additionality of resources, which were contemplated in the proposals evolved by the Latin American countries pursuant to the spirit of the Punta del Este Charter.

Except in regard to the territories of their immediate and special interest, the Western European countries have proven themselves, by and large, insensitive to the needs of the developing countries for ampler and less obstructed access to industrialized markets capable of supplying equipment goods. It is thus not surprising that balance-of-payment problems of the less developed countries vis-à-vis Western Europe are showing signs of recurrent aggravation: the relatively short period of repayment of European development loans would require, for their proper amortization, a much freer access to Western European import markets than is possible under present protectionist and discriminatory policies.

TABLE I[2]

Exports of Primary Products by Industrialized and Nonindustrialized Countries
(1953 and 1957–1960)
In U.S. $ billions, value FOB

	1953	1957	1958	1959	1960
I—Exports of industrialized countries	14.3	19.8	18.5	19.9	22.5[a]
As a percentage of total exports of primary products	45.1	50.1	50.8	50.8	53.1
II—Exports of nonindustrialized countries	17.4	19.7	17.9	19.3	19.9[b]
As a percentage of total exports of primary products	54.9	49.9	49.2	49.2	46.9[c]

[2] Source: GATT L/1595 (30/X/1961).
[a] A growth of 57.3 percent.
[b] A growth of 14.4 percent.
[c] Total exports increased by 33.8 percent.

TABLE II[3]

Price Indexes of Primary Products in International Trade
(1953 = 100)

	1953	1957	1958	1959	1960
Food Products	100	98	94	89	88
Coffee, Tea, and Cocoa	100	97	94	80	76
Agricultural Primary Products	100	101	90	94	96
Minerals	100	114	108	103	101
TOTAL (including Petroleum)	100	102	96	94	93

[3] Source: GATT L/1955/30.10.61.

TABLE III[4]

Indexes of Trade and Prices of Primary Products

Year	Trade Volume Index		Price Index	
	Total	Brazil	Total	Brazil
1953	100	100	100	100
1957	129	103	102	87
1958	128	99	96	79
1959	138	115	94	64
1960	150	120	93	63

[4] Data based on documentos of ECOSOC (CICT, May, 1961).

TABLE IV[5]

Coffee Prices, FOB (Spot New York)
(yearly average)

Year	Santos 4	Index	Manizales	Index	Uganda	Index
1953	57.93	100	59.93	100	47.59	100
1954	79.71	138	80.09	134	57.86	122
1955	57.09	98	64.63	108	38.41	81
1956	58.10	100	73.99	123	33.59	71
1957	56.92	98	63.94	107	34.65	73
1958	48.40	83	52.34	87	38.10	80
1959	36.97	64	45.22	75	29.29	61
1960	36.60	63	44.89	75	20.65	43
1961	36.01	62	43.62	73	18.92	40
1962 (April)	34.08	59	41.40	69	20.13	42

[5] Data based on statistics of the Pan American Coffee Bureau.

TABLE V[6]

Terms of Trade of Coffee
in Relation to U.S. Import Price

Year	U.S. Exp. Prices	Santos 4 Index Prices	Santos 4 Terms of Trade	Manizales Index Prices	Manizales Terms of Trade	Native Uganda Index Prices	Native Uganda Terms of Trade
1953	100	100	100	100	100	100	100
1954	99	136	137	134	135	122	123
1955	100	99	99	108	108	81	81
1956	103	100	97	123	119	71	69
1957	107	98	92	107	100	73	68
1958	106	84	79	87	82	79	75
1959	107	64	60	75	70	60	56
1960	108	63	58	74	69	42	39
1961	110	62	56	72	65	39	35

[6] Based on FAO data.

TABLE VI[7]

Dependence of Some Latin American Countries on Coffee Exports
(% of total exports)

	1953	1954	1955	1956	1957	1958	1959	1960	Average 1951–60
Total Latin America	26.0	24.9	22.1	23.3	20.1	20.7	20.3	19.8	22.8
Brazil	70.7	60.7	59.3	69.5	60.7	55.3	57.2	56.2	62.9
Colombia	82.7	83.7	83.5	79.2	76.3	77.0	76.6	71.7	79.2
Costa Rica	41.9	41.4	46.2	50.2	48.7	55.0	52.2	49.1	45.7
El Salvador	85.5	87.6	85.6	77.5	79.3	72.5	62.9	65.9	78.6
Guatemala	68.5	70.7	70.5	74.5	71.0	72.3	71.0	66.8	70.9
Haiti	65.6	79.0	66.5	70.6	61.1	73.8	54.6	52.2	64.7

[7] Source: Document of the Group on Stabilization of Export Revenues, Organization of American States.

TABLE VII[8]

Total U.S. Nonmilitary Aid to Latin American Coffee-Exporting Countries
Fiscal Years 1953–1962

	Foreign Aid	Percentages of total Latin American coffee exports[a]	Percentages of foreign exchange revenue from coffee[b]
Brazil	1,570.9	55.6	62.9
Colombia	648.8	18.4	79.2
Mexico	486.7	4.8	11.7
El Salvador	37.3	4.7	78.6
Guatemala	148.3	4.1	70.9
Costa Rica	83.1	2.7	45.7
Peru	354.7	1.8	3.2
Ecuador	96.1	1.3	19.7
Venezuela	209.4	1.3	1.6
Nicaragua	58.3	1.1	40.6
Haiti	76.9	1.1	64.7
Dominican Republic	38.5	1.0	18.4
Honduras	40.5	1.7	18.0
Cuba	29.0	0.3	0.9
Panama	92.0	0.0	1.0

[8] Source: GTERE–OEA–Doc. 34.
[a] Based on 1961 exports.
[b] Average 1951–1960.

TABLE VIII

Brazil—Loss in Foreign-Exchange Revenue from Coffee Exports
(in U.S. $ million)

Year	Value of Exports (Current Prices)	Value of Exports (1953 prices)	Loss in Foreign Exchange Revenue
1953	1,090.2	...	...
1954	948.1	763.5	+184.6
1955	843.9	959.7	−115.8
1956	1,029.8	1,176.8	−147.0
1957	845.5	1,001.7	−156.2
1958	687.5	903.6	−216.1
1959	733.0	1,225.9	−492.9
1960	712.7	1,176.8	−464.1
1961	710.4	1,190.8	−480.4
1962	642.7	1,148.8	−506.1
			−2,578.6
			+184.6
			−2,394.0

TABLE IX[9]

Coffee in Brazilian Exports
(1952–1962)

Year	Quantity (bags of 132.276 lb.)	Value (U.S. $1,000)	Value per Bag (U.S. $1.00)	Value per Pound (U.S. ¢)	% of Total Value of Exports
1952	15.8	1,045.3	66.07	49.94	73.7
1953	15.6	1,090.2	70.05	52.96	70.8
1954	10.9	948.1	86.84	65.65	60.7
1955	13.7	843.9	61.62	46.58	59.3
1956	16.8	1,029.8	61.28	46.33	69.5
1957	14.3	845.5	59.05	44.64	60.8
1958	12.9	687.5	53.37	40.34	55.4
1959	17.5	733.0	42.67	32.25	58.0
1960	16.8	712.7	42.38	32.03	56.2
1961	17.0	710.4	41.86	31.64	45.7
1962	16.4	642.7	39.19	29.63	52.0

[9] Sources: USDA, Brazilian Coffee Institute.

TABLE X

Brazil—Coffee Exports
(Value in U.S. $ million)

Years	Hypothetical Value[a]	Actual Value	Difference
1953	1,090.2	...	...
1954	1,136.6	948.1	−188.5
1955	1,048.9	843.9	−205.0
1956	1,288.9	1,029.8	−259.1
1957	1,094.8	845.5	−249.3
1958	987.6	687.5	−300.1
1959	1,355.1	733.0	−622.1
1960	1,286.2	712.7	−573.5
1961	1,301.5	710.4	−591.1
1962	1,258.2	642.7	−615.5
			−3,604.2

[a] Calculated at 58 cents per lb., average price of Santos 4 spot N.Y.

TABLE XI

Latin America—Coffee Exports

Years	Quantity	Actual Value	Average Value of Bags	Value 1953	Difference
1953	6.6	422.4	(64.00)		
1954	5.6	491.8	87.82	358.400	+133.4
1955	6.4	469.7	73.39	409.600	+60.1
1956	6.6	512.4	77.63	422.400	+90.0
1957	7.1	522.2	73.54	454.400	+67.8
1958	8.0	470.7	58.83	512.000	+41.3
1959	7.5	372.0	49.60	480.000	−108.0
1960	7.9	397.6	50.32	505.600	−108.0
1961	7.7	362.8	47.11	492.800	−130.0
					+351.3
					−387.3
					−36.0

TABLE XII

Colombia—Coffee Exports

Year	Quantity	Value (Current prices)	Av. Value per Bag (U.S. $)	Value at 1953 Prices	Difference
1953	6.6	492.2	(74.57)		
1954	5.8	550.2	94.86	432.506	+117.7
1955	5.9	487.3	82.59	439.963	+47.3
1956	5.1	413.1	81.00	380.307	+32.8
1957	4.8	421.1	87.72	357.936	+63.2
1958	5.4	391.0	72.40	402.678	−11.7
1959	6.4	395.0	61.71	477.248	−82.2
1960	5.9	333.0	56.44	439.963	−107.0
1961	5.7	307.8	54.00	425.049	−117.2
					+261.0
					−318.1
					−57.1

On the Need for Historical Perspective[1]

We are in the midst of a nation brought to the very verge of moral, political, and material ruin. Corruption dominates the ballot box, the legislature, the Congress and even touches the ermines of the bench. Business is prostrated; our houses covered with mortgages; labor impoverished; and the land concentrated in the hands of capitalists. The fruits of the toil of millions are boldly stolen to build up . . . fortunes for the few . . . we have witnessed for more than one quarter of a century the struggle of the two great parties for power and plunder. Neither do they now promise any substantial reform . . . they propose to sacrifice our homes, lives and children on the altar of Mammon.

This text is not a description of the turmoil and trials of the present transition in the Congo. It is not a stricture by conservative New York financial papers on the situation of economic chaos which in their view is confronting Latin America. The country described in the above quotation is the United States of America, and the diatribe is nothing less than the platform of the Populist Party in its Omaha convention of July 4, 1892.

Despite the objurgation of the Populist Party, with its singular lack of historical perspective, the United States grew to be a mighty nation with a sound economy and fair standards of social justice.

I wonder whether the United States financial circles as well as the press are not afflicted by a similar lack of historical perspective in examining the Brazilian reality. The conviction that such is the case prompts me to expatiate what I consider to be the deformation of the Brazilian image in this country, and also to comment on prevalent misconceptions concerning the size and burden of foreign-assistance programs when placed in the context of trade relationships. I shall also dwell on the leftist reform movements in Brazil and the Communist problem.

[1] A speech given at the Waldorf Astoria in New York, to the Pan American Society, on December 19, 1962.

THE UNDERESTIMATION OF THE BRAZILIAN PERFORMANCE

The performance of a society both in times of glory and in times of trouble must be judged by various indicators of a political, social, and economic nature. In the case of Brazil an obsessive focusing on the inflationary upsurge has led many analysts to disregard unreflectingly significant achievements in other areas.

With the onset of a profound constitutional crisis, brought about by the resignation of President Quadros, in August, 1961, the nation was faced with a number of priority social objectives. First and foremost was upholding the fabric of an open and democratic society. Second was the preservation of a high rate of economic growth. Third, the attainment of a greater measure of autonomy in development decisions; and fourth, the maintenance of a reasonable degree of price stability.

The first objective appears to have been substantially achieved even in the face of major internal tensions. Brazil is approaching the end of the constitutional crisis with the scheduling for January 6 of the plebiscite to decide on the restoration of the presidentialist regime (which is likely to be the choice of the electorate) or the continuation of parliamentarism.[2]

The second objective is almost as important. For only a dynamic economy can provide the job flexibility, the opportunity for social promotion, and the widening of horizons needed to abate social tensions and make for ultimate viability. What is now the record? For the decade of the 50's as a whole, the Brazilian growth rate—5.8 per year in real terms—was the highest of Latin America. In 1960–1961, despite the political crisis and adverse terms of trade, the increase in the Gross National Product was 7.2 percent. While in 1962 the rate of expansion seems to have abated, there are good prospects that 1963, when heavy investments in electricity and steel will come to fruition, may mark another upsurge in production.

In the history of the recent growth of the Brazilian economy, another important feature is that the expansion throughout the decade of the 50's has been achieved with practically unchanged imported inputs, since imports did not increase, while the real GNP expanded by 56 percent. A comparable performance is hard to find in the nonsocialist

---

[2] The results of the plebiscite of January 6, 1963, confirmed, by a wide margin, the option in favor of the presidentialist regime.

world. For in the majority of the developing countries, economic growth has been accompanied by a more than proportionate increase in imported inputs. In the Brazilian case, the enhancement of the coefficient of autonomous growth has been made possible by the rise of import-substituting industries and particularly by the diversification and increasing sophistication of the domestic production of capital goods. In the last few years an entirely new motor vehicle and shipbuilding industry has been created, steel production has expanded at an annual cumulative rate of 13 percent, and more than 50 percent of the needs for equipment goods are now met by domestic production. In the short run, this rapid pace of import substitution adds to the inflationary pressures of the economy. In the long run, it makes for structural flexibility and renders development decisions less dependent on vicissitudes of foreign trade and aid.

The sharpness of the inflationary advance in Brazil is incontrovertible evidence that we did not succeed in maintaining a reasonable degree of price stability. Nothing is further from my mind than to condone inflation or deny the serious social attrition or economic dislocations that come in its wake. There is in fact a general clamor from all sectors of the population in Brazil for measures to control inflation. Some steps have already been taken, such as the passage of a tax-reform bill designed to increase treasury revenues by a minimum of Cr $130 billion. The Executive has also been authorized to present to Congress a program for reducing nonfixed government expenditures by 45 percent during 1963. The specific tax on electricity consumption has been converted into an "ad valorem" tax to provide noninflationary financing for power programs. Proposals for readjusting public utility, transportation, and fuel rates are under study for enforcement as part of an over-all anti-inflationary program. Much ampler financing of the budget deficit through sale of escalator-clause treasury bills is also contemplated.

While the seriousness of the inflationary problem in Brazil and in many other Latin American countries cannot be denied, it is equally true that the current analysis of this problem on the part of international financial organizations and banking circles in this country is far from balanced. There is in the first place, a tendency to regard inflation from a moral and not a sociological viewpoint, as if it were simply a display of moral laxity and not the result of irresistible distributive pressures (claims on consumption), and growth pressures (claims on

On the Need for Historical Perspective

investments) in an environment characterized by adverse trade conditions for exporters of primary products.

There is, secondly, the view that inflated countries are necessarily violating the principle of self-help. This may be true if inflation is not accompanied by growth and is eating up large foreign resources through overspending on imports. Those are certainly not the characteristics of the Brazilian inflation, where growth has been maintained and the diet of imports has been meager. If anything, this proves self-help. For resources are being squeezed from a poor economy, even though by cruel and brutal means.

These comments are in no way a defense of inflation nor is it claimed that inflation played a causal role in the process of growth. In fact, given an adequate political context and efficient tax administration, economic development can be achieved and has been achieved with only moderate inflationary pressures. These comments are, however, a plea for a balanced view of the problem and for recognition of the Brazilian performance in relation to other important social and political objectives.

The inner workings of the Anglo Saxon mind are often mysterious. Somehow, countries that maintained price stability and fiscal discipline, even when suffering from low growth rates or stagnation, are held up as prime examples of self-help and conformity to the Alliance-for-Progress philosophy. But surely in the philosophy of the Alliance, growth takes precedence over stability; and if self-help means anything it means mobilization of resources, and such mobilization, in turn, cannot be meaningful if it does not translate itself into growth and expansion. These thoughts should make one more sober in words and less harsh in judgment when assessing the economic performance in underdeveloped countries.

I am not overlooking the fact that there is justified apprehension in the United States concerning the dangers of inflation in Latin America. But those certainly miss the point who do not recognize that an even greater danger is stagnation. When there is growth, there is a continuous dilatation of the economic horizon, and the correction of social injustices, though often slow, can be made without social explosion. When there is stagnation there is nothing left but a bitter fight for a share in the common misery. Several countries in Latin America and Asia have suffered both from inflation and stagnation while a few others maintained a stable price level but also did not develop.

In Latin America only two countries have managed in recent years to reconcile moderate inflation with an acceptable rate of economic growth, but even those failed to achieve the rate of expansion of the Brazilian economy in the last decade.

The seriousness of the stagnation problem in Latin America has been pungently underlined in the recent report of the Joint ECLA-OAS Secretariat to the ministerial meeting of the Inter-American Economic and Social Council in Mexico City. While during the period 1950–1957, at least seven of the Latin American countries had attained a 2.5 percent annual rate of per capita growth, it would appear, in the light of available data, that during more recent years—1957–1961—only Brazil managed to accomplish the minimum growth objectives set forth in the Punta del Este Charter.

The Burden of Foreign Assistance in the Context of Foreign Trade

There is now in the United States fatigue and disenchantment about foreign assistance. The *disenchantment* is perhaps based on a false analogy: quick results were attained through massive infusion of funds for European recovery, and no similar speed was or can be attained in the economic-development field, for the job goes beyond the reconstruction of the physical plant and the setting in motion of existing skills. The job is to promote social transformation, to create new skills, and to modernize the whole fabric of society. Quite outside the fact that the scale of resources mobilized for the Alliance of Progress is but a fraction of that poured into Europe, the nature of the task does not lend itself to dramatic short-run achievements.

The *fatigue* stems perhaps from an overestimation of the real burden placed on the American economy by programs of foreign aid to underdeveloped countries in general, and to Latin America in particular. Those programs now absorb less than 1 percent of the GNP as compared to nearly 2 percent taken by the Marshall Plan; and the American economy still has at present underutilized human and plant resources. More important still is a related underestimation of the subtle savings accruing to the consumer-taxpayer from the steady decline, since 1953, of the prices of import for primary products, a decline which in the case of Latin American exports has been sufficiently large to frustrate expected beneficial effects from aid.

This point which tends to be neglected in current discussions has been adequately emphasized in a recent speech by Mr. Edwin Martin,

On the Need for Historical Perspective

Assistant Secretary of State for Inter-American Affairs, given at the Institute of World Affairs, in the University of Southern California:

Between 1953 and 1960 Latin American exports other than oil grew in quantity by 30% but brought in only 4% more foreign exchange. If prices had stayed at 1953 levels, Latin American earnings from exports would have been $1.3 billion larger than they were. You can understand how much difference this would have made.

Their exports are largely products whose prices fluctuate widely in response to small variations of supply. Accordingly, if they had exported much more of those products they would probably have earned less rather than more. Even as it was, the average price in 1961 of coffee and cocoa was only about 60% of the 1953 level, bananas 85%, and fibers—cotton and wool—about 80%. These products alone accounted for one-fourth of Latin American export earnings in that year.

Meanwhile, U.S. wholesale prices—a rough guide to their import costs—had increased 10%.

This 4% increase in export earnings was accompanied by an increase in population of some 20%. Clearly per capita export earnings fell substantially. And since government revenues are greatly affected by both export levels and the amount of imports that export levels permit to be bought, as well as by related domestic business prosperity, they have increasingly fallen short of the demands made upon them.

Mr. Martin has underlined two aspects of the declining trend of Latin American terms of trade. The first is the resulting pressure on the balance of payments, which made it necessary to devote roughly 40 percent of the funds disbursed during the first year of operation of the Alliance for Progress for direct or indirect balance-of-payment loans. If the relationship between aid and trade were placed in proper perspective, the unqualified condemnation of balance-of-payment loans as indicating wastefulness or laxity in aid administration would appear quite irrational. Mr. Martin called attention also to the inflationary effect of declining trends of trade in those cases where tax revenues of the government are heavily dependent on export taxation. A similar effect, it might be added, occurs if the loss of exchange revenue forces a reduction of imports that might otherwise abate the inflationary pressure.

In the last few months a number of objurgations have been heard, both from informed and uninformed sources, concerning the supposed wastefulness of assistance to Brazil in view of persistent inflation and the recurrent balance-of-payment crisis.

In the light of this fact, I might not be regarded as ungracious or impolite if I make some attempt to place the assistance given to Brazil in proper perspective. There is an altogether exaggerated idea concerning the net volume of resources transferred to the Brazilian economy. This results partly from the utilization of gross figures relating to commitments and authorization rather than to actual disbursements, and from disregarding the reverse flow of amortization and interest payments.

A second aspect is the substantial increase in disbursements since the inception of the Alliance for Progress, which coincided with particularly adverse foreign-trade conditions. In *net* terms, and viewed in a long perspective, from 1940 to 1962, the net transfers of United States government assistance to Brazil in various forms—loans, grants, food supplies—from all sources—Eximbank, ICA, AID, Food for Peace, Peace Corps, Social Development Trust Fund, PL 480—have amounted to roughly $1 billion, or to be precise $1,024 million. Spread over the entire period, this would mean less than $50 million per year, although as said before, the net flow of funds increased substantially after the inception of the Alliance for Progress. It can hardly be said that this assistance has been wasted, for this would be inconsistent with the high rate of growth maintained by the Brazilian economy. But the important thing is that in welfare terms the burden of assistance has been greatly reduced by the savings accruing involuntarily to the North American consumer-taxpayer, through cheaper prices paid for our primary exports. A simple calculation will bring this out. If the cumulative value of Brazilian exports at current prices from 1955 to 1961 is adjusted by the terms-of-trade ratio prevailing for the period of 1950–1953, the additional export earnings would have amounted to $1.4 billion in the last six years alone. During the same lapse of time, the accumulated deficit of the Brazilian balance of payments was roughly $966 million, substantially less than the decline in export earnings.

Since there is nothing more dangerous than to overprove a case, I hasten to qualify the meaning of this statement. My purpose *was not* to belittle the good will and forbearance of the U.S. taxpayer, who feels directly the real burden of the tax while his saving as a consumer of Latin American products is distant, unrequested, and diffused. My purpose *was not* to ascribe guilt to the United States for the deterioration of the Latin American terms of trade. For just as the rising prices of primary products from 1949 to 1954 were not due to the generosity of the American trader, the price decline since 1955 does not prove his

On the Need for Historical Perspective

exploitative bent. My purpose *was not* to deny that the betterment of the terms of trade for the industrial producers benefited Europe as well as the United States, and that while the latter endeavors to alleviate the problems of primary producers by foreign-aid programs or by sponsoring commodity agreements such as that dealing with coffee, the Western European countries have dragged their feet both in regard to loan assistance and to the improvement of trade conditions with the underdeveloped countries. My purpose *was not* to imply that there is any moral obligation on the part of the developed nations to make restitution for the gains from trade, although this might be commendable in their own self interest, just as within most industrialized countries protection is given to farm prices in order to maintain markets for industrial goods and to avoid socially painful and politically dangerous income inequalities.

But when all is said and done, the fact remains that there is little justification for a self-righteous attitude on the part of the lending countries, as if inflation and balance-of-payment troubles in Latin America were plain lack of guts or love of vice, and not the symptoms of a difficult travail in the face of adverse winds of trade, impatience of consumers, and confused aspirations for the fruits of progress before the tree has matured to yield.

ON THE PITFALLS OF THE POLITICAL VOCABULARY

Another image deformation results from the loose utilization of the word "Communist" to describe various strains of leftist movement in Latin America in general, and in Brazil in particular. In a pluralistic society, facing the enormous task of reform, there are bound to be profound divergences as to methods and intensity of the required social change.

The left in Brazil encompasses a wide spectrum—the Catholic left; the nationalist left; the utopian socialist apparatus which appears to be losing ground steadily, bitterly split as it is among three factions—the Stalin-Marxist dogmatists, the Khrushchevian revisionists, and a small residuum of the old Trotskyite movement.

It is true that Communism remains a danger, despite its numerical insignificance, because of the frustrations of underdevelopment and the temptation to correct still prevailing social injustices by revolutionary means; because of the uncanny ability of the party for infiltration and sabotage; and because of the Communists' skillful manipulation of popular reform movements, which they seek to twist and poison in order to serve antidemocratic objectives and to disturb the march of development within Western institutions.

But we cannot fight this danger by indiscriminately labelling as Communists all those who favor an enlargement of the area of state ownership or practice the sport of anti-Americanism, wrong as they may be from the viewpoint of maintaining economic efficiency and unfair as they may be in interpreting American motivation and ideals. (Painful as this is, the Americans have to recognize that the price of power is solitude; and that the glory of leadership and wealth breeds not only respect but also resentment.) In particular, one must not defeat the purpose of social reforms—which is at the very core of the Alliance for Progress—by an unwarranted identification of the reformists with the revolutionaries.

It is time to recognize, in any view, that the traditional political vocabulary of right, center, and left is outmoded and quite meaningless in the Brazilian landscape.

It would be better to speak of the *conservatives*, who desire to preserve the status quo; the *reformists*, encompassing a broad political spectrum ranging from right of the center to a large segment of the left, who may disagree on the type and intensity of reforms but agree on the basic postulate that they should be instituted through the democratic mechanism; and finally the *subversives*—who advocate violent change by totalitarian methods—encompassing the Communists, the ultramontane nationalist left, and a small residuum of rightist revolutionaries.

It is time we realize that Communism, as Guy Mollet, the French socialist, once said, is neither to the right nor to the left, but rather to the East.

Some Concluding Words

The changing face of Latin America is full of paradoxes. Some of the countries, relatively stable on the surface and able to maintain satisfactory financial discipline, may conceal explosive elements; while less disciplined countries, exhibiting the superficial turmoil characteristic of pluralistic societies with diffused power, may be endowed with greater resilience and enduring strength.

The crucial criteria are whether the masses are being brought to increased participation in the political process, whether the areas of social promotion exceed the areas of rigidity, and whether the rate of development is sufficient to make the more dynamic groups interested in advancing through the bargaining process rather than through the surgery of revolution.

These factors—much more than banking measurements of creditworthiness, price stability, or budget discipline, so obsessively inspected by lending agencies in Washington—will ultimately determine both the political and the economic viability of the society.

One should not be disturbed by the often hesitant and confused workings of the democratic process, even though at times vitiated by demagoguery and apparently misguided economic policies. For recent history has proved that Communist revolutions have only been successful when projected against authoritarian states, in which access to power is the privilege of a class or a group. (Czechoslovakia was an exception, but their revolution was imposed from without.) Democracies, even when poor and imperfect, have managed to survive, for they never present a target sufficiently rigid to permit a successful revolutionary impact.

Having heard in the last few months so many dire predictions of chaos in the Brazilian economy and so many exhortations on formulas of salvation, I cannot resist the temptation to close this discussion where it began—by recalling the Populist platform's castigation of the American impending economic disaster and political disintegration at the turn of the century.

Let us not confuse an historical perspective, which may bring recipes of wisdom, with an hysterical perspective, which may bring decisions in anger and poison the wells of understanding.

The Dilemmas of Trade and Aid[1]

In a world which, for both political and ethical reasons, has committed itself to closing the gap in standards of living between the peoples of industrial and nonindustrial countries, the problem of economic development ceased being a matter of concern to national governments alone, to become one of the thorniest issues in the relations among nations, especially between developed and underdeveloped countries. The notion that the rich nations have the responsibility to help the development of the poor ones—together with a better understanding of the relationship between trade and economic development—has brought to the agenda of practically every major international conference the problems of trade and aid.

In the lengthy and sometimes bitter dialogue between the two interested groups of nations some very valid points of disagreement, as well as some spurious ones, have emerged. Among the latter, one of the most relevant concerns the role of trade and aid in the process of economic development of less-developed countries. The habit of viewing international aid as an act of philanthropy or moral condescendence tends to leave the receiving countries with a lingering feeling of humiliation, and causes the industrial countries to assume a self-righteous attitude of resentment at what they consider a rather lax or even ungrateful behavior on the part of less-developed countries. As a result, political resistance to foreign-assistance programs increases among the industrial countries. On the other hand, developing countries justify their demands for aid by picturing international assistance, at least in part, as a compensation for unfair treatment received from industrial countries, whether as colonial powers or as trade partners. In extreme manifesta-

[1] An address given at the World Trade and Market Conference, Albany, New York, on November 13, 1963.

tions, some groups in the industrialized countries appear to regard aid purely as a philanthropic exercise; while in the receiving countries hostile-minded groups see it as a form of "conscience money."

I shall not dwell on a debate that has often generated more heat than light. My brief purpose would be first to comment on some of the dilemmas of aid programs, as an introduction to what I feel is the real core of our inquiry, namely the relationship between trade and aid.

A lot has been said, often in a self-righteous tone, in the United States and in Western Europe about the inadequate behavior of the recipient countries—laxity in self-help measures, sluggishness in promoting social reforms, fiscal and balance-of-payments indiscipline. It may be refreshing, though not perhaps pleasant, to look at the reverse side of the coin and try to focus on the problem from the point of view of the developing countries—in short, to cause the *reformable*, beset by hesitancy and contradictions—to look critically at the *reformers*.

THE DILEMMAS OF FOREIGN AID

The first contradiction we meet is the glib enthusiasm of the industrialized countries in preaching structural reforms—social and economic—in the developing countries, often as a pre-condition for aid—while overlooking their own responsibility to make structural changes themselves (particularly in trade policies) designed to assist the developing countries in diversifying their productive patterns and decreasing their need for, and reliance on, foreign assistance. It is no doubt paradoxical that some of the rich countries are sincerely convinced of the generosity of their aid programs designed to foster the development of the emerging nations, while at the same time placing major obstacles in the way of exports which would provide the poor countries with the indispensable means for development. It is true that poor countries will not advance much without far-reaching cultural and social transformations. It is equally true that genuine cooperation on the part of the industrialized nations would require them to accept structural changes and internal adjustments to render their markets accessible to the developing countries. Structural change should not be a one-way street. And aid must not be "conscience money" paid by the industrialized countries to eschew the anguishing decision to open their markets for exports from the poor countries.

The second dilemma involved in foreign-assistance programs, a dilemma which lurks unrecognized beneath the stormy surface of recent aid debates in the United States, is that the objective of accelerating institutional reforms in the receiving countries (such as the agrarian reform or the tax reform) may in the short run be incompatible with other desirable objectives, such as the creation of a favorable climate for private investment or the stabilization of price levels. The reason is clear. The more drastic the pace of fiscal and agrarian reform, the greater the likelihood that the propertied classes which now form the bulk of private entrepreneurial and investor groups will feel fretful, aggravated, and suspicious at the winds of change. Similarly, the prescription for social justice is likely to stimulate wage and welfare revindications which complicate the task of inflation control and price stabilization. This does not mean of course that the objectives of social reform and social justice in the developing countries are either incorrect or postponable. They are neither. In fact, in the long run all of the objectives mentioned are not only compatible but mutually self-reinforcing. The incompatibility is purely a short-run matter. But, as Lord Keynes said, in the long run we shall all be dead.

If the decision is rightly taken—and this seems to be the mood in present congressional discussion of the aid bill—to press the case for fundamental reforms in Latin America, we ought not to hope sanguinely for a simultaneous improvement in the climate for private investment, or to take to the warpath if the tension and bitterness of reform movements destroy the passivity and predictability of conventional economic attitudes in relation to foreign investment. More often than not, irrational and emotional attitudes during periods of fast structural change give way to a more relaxed posture when a higher degree of social integration and a more equitable pattern of income distribution are finally attained.

Raucous nationalism and hostility to foreign creditors were rampant in the United States at a historical period not unlike the present one in Latin America and in other underdeveloped regions, which are trying passionately to break down an obsolete social order and affirm a new national image.

A sense of historical perspective, a perceptive hierarchy of priorities, a compassionate understanding of the tensions of change are needed if those who intend to use foreign aid as an instrument of reform are not to ruin the cause of reform.

AID AND TRADE IN A PROPER PERSPECTIVE

This brings me to the third and main object of my disquisition—the relationship between trade and aid in the context of economic development.

The initial observation to be made is that trade plays a vastly larger role than aid in providing the developing countries with the wherewithal needed for financing the importation of developmental goods and services. In a typical year, 1960, combined exports of the developing countries valued over $30 billion, while all foreign aid plus foreign investments did not reach $8 billion.

We must recognize, however, that aid may have a qualitative importance much greater than its quantitative impact, for it permits resources to be directed purposively for projects of economic development and diversification, while trade revenues may be used to perpetuate unbalanced production patterns.

Another point to be stressed is that the volume of aid has been too small in comparison with the needs of developing countries and has not even filled the gap left by the deterioration of the trade position of the underdeveloped countries in the late 50's and early 60's. This is particularly true in the case of Latin America. Data of the Grace report, prepared by a group of businessmen as a contribution to the discussion of the Clay Committee, indicate that the increase in United States aid in 1961—the first year of the Alliance for Progress—covered only 22 percent of the deterioration of the balance-of-payment position of the seven major countries in Latin America, by comparison with the yearly average for the period 1950–1956.

In a deep sense it might be said that there has been no net transfer of resources from the United States to Latin America from 1956 through 1963. Thus perhaps "aid programs" have been a misnomer. We ought to be using other wording, such as "partial compensatory financing," to describe programs of financial assistance for Latin America. Such a phrase would have the advantage of dispelling the impression that aid programs are placing a heavy burden on the American economy—a feeling which is subjectively correct from the viewpoint of the individual taxpayer but inaccurate for the over-all economy—and the even greater advantage of forestalling frustrations arising from overblown expectations of dramatic improvements in Latin America.

I do not want, "of course," to imply that there is any moral obligation on the part of the United States or other industrialized countries to recompose the level of exchange earnings of Latin America in the early 50's, or to support any specific level of prices of primary products, or to endorse overproduction of any commodity. What I merely imply is that if the American economy in the early 50's—an economy with a per capita income 25 percent lower than at present—could without any hardship (in fact with less underemployment and a higher rate of growth than today) provide a better remuneration for Latin American exports, surely the mere recomposition, through aid programs, of the level of exchange earnings of the early 1950's should not be regarded either as a wasteful burden or a magic leverage capable of inducing sudden reform and growth in Latin America.

In this light, the argument that pictures foreign-assistance programs as a source of balance-of-payment problems for the aid-giving countries appears fallacious. The fact is that in the last decade the gold and foreign-exchange reserves of the less-developed countries remained stagnant despite the increase in world trade, and in Latin America there has been an actual decrease in the absolute level of reserves.

Whatever the conception one may have of the role and burden of aid in the context of trade, prospects are not bright for increased foreign assistance in the future; and if such increases are to occur they may be so riddled with conditions and restraints that one might legitimately fear that the administration of aid programs will be cumbersome and politically frustrating. Hence the imperative need for the developing countries to devote increasing attention to trade as a means to pay for the productive resources and consumer goods they must import.

Obstacles to the Trade of Developing Countries

Unfortunately, however, about 90 percent of the exports of less-developed countries are primary products, the demand for which tends to grow at a very slow pace. This tendency is well illustrated by the fact that during the period 1904–1913 the consumption of primary products (exclusive of gold) in the United States represented 22.6 percent of the GNP, while in 1944–50 it had already fallen to 12.5 percent.

Furthermore, the international trade in primary commodities has displayed a marked instability, as exemplified by the fact that in the postwar period export fluctuations from trend have averaged 30–40 percent more for the primary exporting countries than for the industrial ones. Those wide swings around an already unsatisfactory trend have put an

The Dilemmas of Trade and Aid

additional strain on the underdeveloped countries' limited exchange resources, thereby thwarting both their economic development and their efforts at economic stability.

In addition to those problems of a more technical nature, the pattern of trade in primary products has been changing adversely for the less-developed countries. Between 1953 and 1960 over-all exports of primary products rose by 34 percent, but the underdeveloped countries, which accounted for 55 percent of world commodity exports in 1953, saw their participation shrink to 47 percent in 1960, while the industrialized countries raised theirs from 45 to 53 percent in the same period.

Of special significance for the future of exports of less-developed countries are the protective policies adopted by most industrial nations, through tariffs, quantitative restrictions, and subsidies. Such policies have, in many cases, attained a level which is unjustifiably detrimental to primary producing countries or have even turned, in practice, into export promotion programs.

Even where no protection of domestic production is involved, internal taxes and other measures often tend to discourage consumption, thereby reducing trade. The taxes levied by some European countries on coffee and cocoa are well-known examples.

In view of the foregoing facts, it is clear that if the industrial countries wish to be consistent with their avowed policy objective of fostering the economic development of nonindustrial countries, they must accept a substantial degree of liberalization in primary-commodities trade. Even such a liberalization, however, may not raise sufficiently the export earnings of primary-exporting countries, both because of the slow growth in the demand for those products and because of the deterioration in the terms of trade between those countries and the industrial ones. According to IMF estimates "the ratio of the prices of primary products to those of manufactured goods has declined by more than 20% in the course of the 50's."

Under the circumstances, it becomes necessary that less-developed countries diversify their exports of primary commodities and strive to export also some manufactures. Here again the trade policies of developed countries are a hindrance rather than a help. First, there is a general tendency to impose higher tariffs on products with a higher degree of processing. Secondly, when less-developed countries become efficient producers of certain manufactures, they can only reap the fruits of their competitive position to the extent that they do not interfere with the trade of traditional producers. Beyond that point, it is claimed that new producers are disrupting the market and the right to impose restrictions on trade is invoked by those who feel their interests are being jeopardized.

A striking example of this kind of attitude is the textile agreement, signed last year under the sponsorship of GATT. While one might still accept the idea of temporary restrictions to trade to be applied for a reasonable and clearly stated period of time, in order to permit traditional producers to adjust themselves to new conditions, one can hardly feel in sympathy with a device apparently destined to freeze an outdated pattern of trade.

One reflection of the obstacles found by the underdeveloped countries in marketing their exports is the exaggerated reliance that they are placing on often uneconomical import-substituting industries; in the face of an unreasonable market obstruction abroad, developing countries are turning, as a "no-alternative policy," to inward-oriented patterns of development, which though at times detrimental to over-all world productivity, do offer them the promise of escaping the confines of stagnation.

It is fair to recognize that the United States has shown a more understanding and more liberal attitude toward imports from the developing countries than has Western Europe. Europe is veering toward a protective and discriminatory trade policy that will undoubtedly hamper the access of poor countries to their markets. Even the United States, however, still maintains several types of restrictions bearing on primary products from Latin America, the removal of which might result, according to estimates of the National Planning Association, in increasing export earnings for that area ranging from $850 million to $1.7 billion per year, a sum equivalent to or larger than the outlays envisaged for the Alliance for Progress.

The Right to Trade Versus the Favor of Aid

If I have laid so much stress on the problems of falling prices and shrinking trade opportunities, it is because I think that there has been altogether too much emphasis, in the current debate in the United States, on the role, the magnitude, and the criteria of foreign aid, with such overtones that cannot but leave on the lips of the receiving countries a bitter taste of humiliation. I am sure that the Latin American countries would much prefer, if they could, to obtain through trade

The Dilemmas of Trade and Aid

rather than through aid the foreign exchange needed for their economic development.

As Professor Sidney Dell, of the Department of Economic Affairs of the United Nations, has put with burning vigor in a recent book: "The basic economic issue between the developed and underdeveloped countries is trade, not aid. It involves the entire role of the underdeveloped countries in the world economy and not simply the crumbs that may fall to them from the tables of the rich. It concerns the earned income that should belong to the underdeveloped countries as of right, and not the charity which is theirs only at the discretion of, and subject to, the passing whims and predilections of others."[2]

[2] Sidney Dell, *Trade Blocs and Common Markets* (London: Constable, 1963), p. 134.

Economic Development and Inflation, with Special Reference to Latin America[1]

THE CATCHWORDS: "MONETARISM" AND "STRUCTURALISM"

I ought to start this discussion with an act of contrition. For I feel I deserve to pay penance for having coined the words *monetarism* and *structuralism* to describe the current debate in Latin America on the relationship of inflation to economic development and on both the diagnosis and therapy of inflation.[2] When impounded by catchwords, some concepts become unduly rigidified and areas of discrepancy are often exaggerated by the artificial semantic contrast.

I feel that the label is, by a twist of irony, particularly unfair to the Latin American monetarists, a group of economists with whom I have great affinity. In fact, I never intended to use *monetarism* to define a school of thought that believes exclusively in monetary policy for either the diagnosis or the therapy of inflation. Monetarists might perhaps better be called *fiscalists*, since they also lay great emphasis on fiscal adjustments. There are several reasons why it would be absurd to interpret restrictively the catchword *monetarism*, when it is applied to policy making in Latin America and underdeveloped countries in general. Firstly, due to the primitive organization of monetary markets and their lack of responsiveness to open-market measures and interest-rate fixation, the role of monetary policies in underdeveloped countries is likely to be smaller than in the typical industrialized society. Secondly, a major causal factor in the inflation in Latin America is governmental

---

[1] A speech delivered at the Third Annual Meeting of Directors of Economic Training Institutes, sponsored by the Organization for Economic Cooperation and Development, Berlin-Tegel, September 9–11, 1963.

[2] Roberto de Oliveira Campos, "Two Views on Inflation in Latin America," in Albert O. Hirschman, *Latin American Issues: Essays and Comments* (New York: Twentieth Century Fund, 1961), p. 69.

deficit spending; accordingly, the therapy has to be sought largely in the fiscal field.

The label *structuralist* is a lot more attractive. It gives an impression of fundamentalism, which becomes even more appealing because of the recognized need for structural transformation during the process of development. But again the concept has now been abusively enlarged to cover just about every type of economic rigidity whether short run or long term, whether autonomous or induced by the very inflation that the structuralists seek to explain.[3] Thus, in addition to the two basic structural inelasticities—food production and capacity to import—other elements of rigidity, now described as *structural*, are the pattern of income distribution and the instability of government revenues in face of rigid government expenditures.[4]

Of this list of factors, the inelasticity of agricultural production can best claim to represent a structural bottleneck, in view of its direct relationship with the problem of land tenure (the blunting of market incentives through price controls on agricultural products also may hold part of the explanation for the sluggishness of food supply).

As regards the capacity to import, the basic argument is that the income elasticity of imports is higher for the underdeveloped primary-producing countries than for the more advanced ones. This results in a chronic inadequacy of the export revenue of the less-developed countries for financing needed imports, creating pressure for inflationary import substitutions, as a deliberate development policy to maintain internal growth in the face of a sluggish export sector.[5] The phenome-

---

[3] Professor Hirschman has recently broached the interesting idea that structuralism may not be an economic theory at all but simply a device for problem solving, using the excuse of inflation to force the solution of other problems—such as land tenure or tax reform—which otherwise would not come into focus for decision making. "Making the Best of Inflation," notes for the Rio de Janeiro Conference on Inflation and Development in Latin America, January, 1963.

[4] See Joseph Grunwald, "The Structuralist School on Price Stabilization and Economic Development: The Chilean Case," in Hirschman, *Latin American Issues*, p. 95.

[5] An example of the interplay of autonomous and induced rigidities can be found in import-substitution policies. The structural bottleneck of inadequate import capacity creates pressure for import substitution. But import substitution itself creates new rigidities because (a) the import of raw materials, fuel, replacement parts, *etc.*, is more difficult to compress than the import of finished goods, particularly because of the social risks of unemployment in the industries; (b) the new import-substituting industries often need high levels of protection; (c) in view of the narrow domestic markets those industries tend to assume monopolistic features. See Grunwald, "The Structuralist School," p. 113.

non undoubtedly exists but whether one should describe it as a structural factor is a moot question, because the elasticity of exports can be vitally affected by exchange-rate policies which lie close to the monetary sphere. Distribution of income and government expenditures are clearly inscribed in the monetary and fiscal area and only through rather elastic semantic exercises can they be called structural factors.

Other categories of factors mentioned by the structuralists, which although nonstructural in nature are also described as incapable of control by monetary policies, are *circumstantial factors,* such as political upheavals, physical catastrophes, exogenous increases in import prices, or irrational government intervention; and *propagation factors,* of which the most important is the wage-spiral mechanism.

The Spurious Controversy

The controversy between monetarists and structuralists in Latin America has been exaggerated beyond all bounds. While rather virulent in theoretical disquisitions, it narrows down substantially when practical policy recommendations have to be formulated. Economists of the structuralist persuasion, for instance, had a preponderant influence in the preparation of a recent anti-inflationary program in Brazil, embodied in a Three-Year Development Plan (Plano Trienal), but their pharmacopoeia presented practically no innovations on prior stabilization efforts planned by economists of the monetarist persuasion. Not only were the remedies and policies quite similar, but the failure of the program came with the same speed, bearing evidence to the fact that stabilization is much less a technical problem than a political one.

One cruel fact, that the structuralists must face when entrusted with policy responsibilities outside the academic wards, is that structural adjustments inevitably take a long time, while the combat to inflation, if it is to succeed, needs fairly quick, visible results. Such results can be obtained much more expeditiously (though often at the cost of painful side effects) through the demand side—via monetary and fiscal policies—than through the supply side (unless foreign aid is available in unlimited amounts). I do not, of course, deny that the purely monetary or fiscal solution may not be durable or consistent with stable growth, unless adjustments are also made on the supply side. The truth is that in the short run all structuralists when entrusted with policy-making responsibilities become monetarists, while all monetarists are, in the long run, structuralists. Thus, we might jocosely define a mone-

Economic Development and Inflation

tarist as a structuralist in a hurry and a structuralist as a monetarist without policy-making responsibility.

Let us try to determine, at this stage, what the controversy is not. It is not a quarrel between economists or policy-makers who recognize the existence of structural rigidities and those who do not. All recognize that structural problems do exist. It is not between those who favor economic growth and development and those who do not. It is not between those who advocate an economic policy which permits the economy to grow and those who advocate a restrictive monetary policy in an attempt to hold down the money supply and keep prices absolutely constant.[6]

The basic controversy lies in the tendency of economists of the structuralist persuasion to view monetary expansion and inflation as unavoidable features of structural change and economic growth in Latin America, and correlatedly to claim that the attempt to avoid monetary expansion and inflation will only hamper structural changes and economic growth. If other descriptions are needed, one might say that the structuralists would hold that the permissiveness of the monetary and fiscal policy of the monetary authorities is simply a reflection of exogenous factors, particularly the decline in import capacity, while the monetarists would hold that this fatalistic result is not inevitable and that inflation cannot be blamed exclusively or even predominantly on exogenous factors, but rather on the "policies of inaction" pursued by most of the Latin American governments.

Another spurious presentation of the controversy is the view that monetarists in Latin America are slavishly following monetary tenets of classical liberalism by adhering strictly to the quantity theory in money and banking, to free-trade views in matters of international trade, to nonintervention doctrines insofar as government activities are concerned, and generally by ascribing lower priority to development than to stabilization and by neglecting the special problems of structural underemployment or unemployment in underdeveloped countries. This fabricated image is quite unfair to the economists of the monetarist persuasion, most of whom are ready to point out the shortcomings of the traditional theory of international trade, and many of whom are adept at planning or programming. They certainly would reject any idea of subordinating growth to stabilization, since they hold

[6] See Jorge del Canto's comments on the topic, "Synthesis of the Experience of the Latin American Countries," in the Conference on Inflation and Development in Latin America, Rio de Janeiro, January, 1963.

that a reasonable degree of monetary stability is useful precisely because it is conducive to structural transformation and growth and the maintenance of external balance.[7]

The Real Controversy

The Monetarist View on Inflation and Growth

Apart from a small current of thought that approaches the question of inflation and development in terms of value judgments, and that, by questioning the social advantage of inflation-financed development, tends to ascribe high social priority to stabilization, the bulk of the monetarists in Latin America appear to recognize the social priority of development, while insisting that continued and stable growth can best be attained in an environment of monetary stability. Their position can be summarized as follows:

1) Inflation's only possible contributions to growth would derive (a) from the forced saving mechanism, through which the decline in real wages due to rising prices and the wage lag would increase investible profits (thus inflation would act as a disguised taxation on consumers and savers to the benefit of investors); (b) from the assumption that the pressure of inflationary demand would permit a fuller utilization of manpower and resources, while conversely the attempt to combat inflation by wiping out excess demand might bring employment and resource utilization down to the level permitted by bottleneck factors; (c) from the assumption that inflation would stimulate bold entrepreneurship and reward investors at the expense of conservative savers or *rentiers*. Against these supposed advantages, the monetarists raise a formidable number of qualifications. The forced savings device can act only temporarily, for discontinuous inflation, but has its efficacy lowered or destroyed when inflation is chronic and becomes a part of the expectation of wage earners, who devise defense stratagems to prevent a decline in real wages. It is true that in dual societies, in which because of institutional factors real wages in some urban industries are set above the limit of marginal productivity, it is possi-

[7] For a summary of the alleged irrelevance of monetarism in Latin America because of the adherence of monetarists to outmoded "classical" tenets, see Dudley Seers, "Inflation and Growth: the heart of the controversy," paper presented to the Conference on Inflation and Growth in Latin America, Rio de Janeiro, January, 1963. Mr. Seers appears to construct a straw man and then proceed with great gusto to destroy it.

ble—because of the continuous attraction of underemployed rural labor to the city and the relative rigidity of factoral proportions of labor and capital in modern technology—to depress the real urban wage for protracted periods; this, however, only prolongs a little bit the usefulness of the forced savings mechanism but does not guarantee its continuity. Such transfer of resources as may take place from consumers to the government or to investors may be offset by the luxury consumption of the entrepreneurial group, by lower efficiency of government investments, or by bottlenecks in the import capacity. While inflation encourages the adventurous entrepreneur, it tends to discourage risk taking in basic enterprises of a long maturation period.

2) Inflation discourages the inflow of foreign capital and renders more difficult the absorption of financing from foreign governments and institutional organizations.

3) Inflation tends to impair the qualitative composition of investments. It discourages investments in basic industries and infra-structural services which either are price controlled, or require long gestation periods, or both. It weakens or prevents the creation of credit and capital markets and stimulates speculative investments in inventories.[8]

4) The structural thesis exaggerates the two basic alleged rigidities: the inelasticity of the food supply and the inelasticity of exports. The reasoning of the structuralists starts from the premise of a total sectoral incompressibility of prices, so that any upward price pressure would result in a rise in the general price level. Thus the pressure of population growth and rising urban incomes would tend to raise, through a chain-reaction mechanism, first the price of agriculture goods, secondly the general price level, and thirdly wages, thus creating an inflationary spiral of a structural nature. Similarly, the inelasticity of world demand for primary exports would tend to lower the export capacity below import requirements for growth, rendering necessary an accelerated process of import substitution. But, at least initially, import substitution tends to be inflationary because of the relative inefficiency of the new

[8] These results need not necessarily occur. For a different view, see Werner Baer, "Inflation and Economic Efficiency in Brazil," a paper presented at the Rio de Janeiro Conference on Inflation and Growth, January, 1963. Mr. Baer stresses that inflation in Brazil for the past decades has not resulted in a patent deterioration in resource allocation, probably because businessmen anticipating inflation were able in advance to make the necessary correction in their plans for price changes. The results are, however, inconclusive, for other factors such as improvement in the terms of trade or corrective government intervention may have permitted a better allocation of investments than would be possible under inflationary conditions unaccompanied by such offsetting factors.

industries during the learning period, this cost pressure being aggravated by the need for exchange devaluations in an attempt to restore external balance. The monetarists would argue that the alleged structural inelasticity of food supplies is often not structural at all. It stems frequently from the fact that the administrative control of food prices, designed to protect the urban consumer, cuts off the agricultural producer from price and market stimuli, so that the inelasticity of food supply, rather than being an inherent structural characteristic, may be a distortion induced by administrative controls. While in some cases the structure of land tenure would prevent in any event the diffusion of market incentives, rendering structural reform a precondition for increasing food production, this situation occurs only rarely. As to industrial-import substitution, while it is not denied that it carries a built-in inflationary pressure—at least if the industrial expansion takes place at constant cost—the cost-push arising therefrom has been grossly exaggerated. Thus, assuming that imports for a typical underdeveloped country represent 10 percent of the national product, that real income is rising at 6 percent per annum, that exports are stationary and that the income elasticity deriving from demand for imported products equals 2 percent and, finally, that the needed customs protection for the national substitutes is 100 percent—all of those factors would not entail a price increase above 1.2 percent per annum, a margin vastly surpassed in the inflated economies of Latin America.[9]

The monetarist approach has, curiously enough, been attacked from two conflicting vantage points. It is argued, on the one hand, that it is too strong because controls will restrain investment, generating unemployment and losses in real output, thus not only aggravating the supply problem but also arousing political instability. Some argue, on the other hand, that it is too weak, because without the leverage of fiscal policies it does not really control excess demand nor go to the heart of structural and institutional problems.

Four points may be readily granted. First, the only meaningful interpretation of the monetarist approach is that it encompasses not only the use of traditional monetary weapons—the efficacy of which is by definition very limited in the rather primitive financial markets characteristic of the less-developed countries—but also of fiscal policies. Sec-

[9] For an illuminating discussion of the assumptions underlying the structuralist thesis, see Mario Henrique Simonsen, "A inflação no Brasil," in *A Economia Brasileira e suas perspectivas, Análise e Perspectiva Econômica* (May, 1963), pp. 208–214.

Economic Development and Inflation

ond, the effectiveness of monetary weapons, *stricto sensu,* is considerably greater in the case of *demand inflation* than of *cost inflation.* This is particularly true if the problem is that of a wage spiral, where the reduction of the quantity of money may stop the rise in prices but *only* at the expense of employment.[10] Third, monetary tools, as distinct from fiscal policies, are inappropriate when the problem is to curb consumption (which can only be achieved via fiscal policies), the effectiveness of monetary restraints being greater if the objective is to contain investment. Fourth, monetary policies have an asymmetrical effect; through a combination of quantitative and qualitative credit controls it is possible to orient a selective expansion of certain economic sectors, but it is much harder to enforce a selective restriction of undesirable sectors.[11]

The conclusions resulting from these observations are that monetary weapons, though indispensable ingredients in anti-inflationary programs, have to be used in prudent combination with fiscal policies. The shortcomings to their application arise not only from asymmetrical effects—they affect investment more than consumption and their efficiency is greater in reducing demand than costs—but from the limited organization and limited responsiveness of money and credit markets in the less-developed countries. Fiscal policies, particularly when designed to curb luxury consumption by taxation of wealthier groups so as to raise the marginal tax above the average rate, have undoubtedly a fundamental role to play in anti-inflation programs.

The applicability of monetary policies depends, of course, on the speed desired in checking inflation and on the degree of flexibility of the wage pattern and labor organization. The latter factor is a major determinant of the possibility of utilization of credit controls without untoward unemployment effects.

The Structuralist View

The structuralist school stresses the "structural vulnerability" of Latin American economies to inflation because of two alleged basic rigidities.

---

[10] See Arthur Lewis, "Closing Remarks" at the Conference on Inflation and Growth in Latin America, Rio de Janeiro, January, 1963. According to Lewis, the wage spiral is a political problem arising from political tensions in the society and incapable of purely economic solution.

[11] For an interesting discussion on the advantages and limitations of monetary policy in Latin America, see Javier Marquez, "Política Monetário-Fiscal como elemento anti-inflacionista." Paper for the Rio de Janeiro Conference on Inflation and Growth.

The first is the slow and unstable rate of export growth, which is held to be chronically inadequate to support the needed rate of development; the sluggish growth rate makes necessary a continuous and sharp effort of import substitution, creating a cost-push because of the substitution effort itself. The instability of the growth rate in turn creates occasional contraction of government tax revenues arising from exports, precisely when government expenditures need to be increased to offset the depressant effect of the stagnation or recession of the export sector. Finally, the trend toward deterioration of the trade in primary products creates an additional complication, further limiting the potential for growth of the export income, and reinforcing the trend toward periodical exchange-rate devaluation. The second basic rigidity is the inelasticity of agricultural production, due largely to defective patterns of land tenure which decrease the responsiveness of food production to price stimuli.

The cost-push in Latin American economies would thus come from a fourfold direction: cost of import substitution, rise in agricultural prices, deterioration of the terms of trade, and exchange-rate devaluation.

Fortified with these tenets, the structuralists proceed to inveigh against what they call the "orthodox" monetary policies advised by the International Monetary Fund, which in their view do not go to the heart of the problem—structural change—and have depressant effects manifested in a decreased level of investment, in the contraction of the private sector due to the incompressibility of the public sector, and in the deflationary effects of unemployment and the wage lag. Thus stability is achieved only at the expense of growth.

While the structuralists are very articulate in their diagnosis of Latin American inflation and in their strictures on monetarism, they are far less explicit on practical policy recommendations. These do not go usually beyond the expression of pious hopes for structural changes, which because of their long-run nature are not serviceable recipes for the short-run cure of inflation. The structuralist tends, therefore, to advocate gradualism in anti-inflationary programs and to postulate an increase in foreign aid and international financing as major factors in helping to buy time for the needed structural changes.

One of the most cogent and articulate criticisms of the structuralist interpretation of Latin American inflation has been put forward recently by Arthur Lewis in his "Closing remarks at the Conference on Inflation and Growth in Latin America," convened in January, 1963, in

Economic Development and Inflation

Rio de Janeiro. Lewis' initial and important contribution is to stress the difference between *self-liquidating inflation* and *spiral inflation*, the first being relevant and the second irrelevant for economic development. Through *self-liquidating inflation* limited policy objectives can be attained, such as altering permanently the distribution of income in favor of investment. The *spiral inflation*, on the other hand, does not serve any growth objective but is rather a political phenomenon, arising from tensions in the society.

The *first* of Lewis' strictures questions the allegedly inevitable sluggishness of the export sector of primary-producing countries. He mentions that between 1950 and 1960 the quantum of trade in primary products grew by 6 percent, only slightly under the rate of growth of manufactured exports, which was 7 percent. While Lewis is right in excoriating the excessive importance attributed by the structuralist school to the structural sluggishness of the export sector in Latin America, he dismisses altogether too glibly the trade problem, which is real. In particular, he overlooks the fact that part of the statistical expansion of exports of primary products in the last decade did not come from the underdeveloped countries but from the industrialized countries. The latter expanded their export of primary products by 57 percent while the former did so by only 14 percent. Thus not only did world trade in manufactures expand at a faster rate, but the lion's share of primary exports was taken by the industrialized countries themselves. Latin American exports also have been greatly affected by a price decline since 1953. While world trade grew in volume by 50 percent between 1953 and 1960, raw material prices declined by 7 percent. Brazil expanded its volume of exports by 20 percent in this period, while unit prices fell by 37 percent. The trade experience with which Professor Lewis is most familiar is that of the sheltered trade area of the British Commonwealth countries. But Latin America was for all practical purposes, until the recent creation of LAFTA, an unsheltered trade area, and the GATT report on "Trends in International Trade" presents conclusive evidence that trade within sheltered areas has been expanding at a substantially faster rate than the trade of unsheltered areas.

Just as Professor Lewis appears to minimize unduly the importance of the decline in the import capacity of Latin America, the structuralists of ECLA overestimate its explanatory and causal role in the process of inflation. As Professor Grunwald has pointed out, despite a decline in the export quantum over the last decade, the Latin American countries managed to maintain or even to increase their import quantum by depletion of exchange reserves and/or increases in international indebtedness.[12]

It is true that such action does not quite solve the problem, particularly in those countries where the decline in export activity requires compensatory government policies for domestic expansion, or where fiscal revenues are greatly dependent on export taxation. But the brunt of the argument is taken. The two main weaknesses of the structuralist view on trade are, then, that some of the sluggishness in the export growth is not really structural but results plainly from a failure, because of over-valued exchange rates, to exploit export opportunities that may still exist; and that the import quantum has been maintained, on the average, for Latin America, despite the decline in export revenues, so that there has been no inflationary decrease in the availability of imported goods.

The *second* stricture of Professor Lewis concerns the wage push. He tends to deny any special characteristic to the Latin American wage scene, as compared to other underdeveloped regions more successful in controlling inflation; he also writes off the wage spiral in Latin America as simply a political problem, resulting from the low degree of sympathy of trade unions for their governments. It is impossible to deny, however, that there are vast differences between Latin America and the underdeveloped regions of Africa or Asia in a number of respects. There is less surplus labor in Latin America, the degree of labor organization is greater, there is more responsiveness to Western consumption habits and less passivity in claiming social benefits. Even within Latin America, there are substantial regional differences, the difficulty of preventing a wage spiral being directly related to the degree of labor-union organization, which seems greater in Argentina and Chile, much lower in Mexico, Peru, and Colombia, while Brazil holds an intermediate position.

The *third* stricture of Professor Lewis concerns the alleged rigidity of agricultural production. He is right in pointing out that pressure on food supplies is not peculiar to the underdeveloped countries of Latin America and that structuralists underestimate the possibility of corrective adjustments by increasing the propensity to export or by reducing the propensity to import.

What might be said by way of conclusion is that the basic flaws in

---

[12] Grunwald, "Invisible Hands in Inflation and Growth," p. 11, paper submitted to the Rio de Janeiro Conference on Inflation and Growth, January, 1963.

Economic Development and Inflation

the structuralist argument seems thus to be (a) that no separation is made between autonomous structural rigidities and induced rigidities resulting from price or exchange controls or mismanaged government intervention; (b) that the quantitative importance of the cost-push generated by import substitution, or by losses in import capacity through the decline in terms of trade, is greatly exaggerated. While these factors might account for a moderate inflationary pressure, they are of little use to explain the massive and chronic inflation in Latin America.

THE INTERNATIONAL MONETARY FUND'S STABILIZATION PROGRAM IN LATIN AMERICA

The strictures of the structuralist school against the "orthodox," largely monetarist, approach of the IMF to stabilization programs in Latin America have played a useful role in fostering a critical reexamination of the Fund's position, a reexamination all the more needed as most of those programs resulted in failure, indicating either their theoretical incorrectness or their political irrelevance for the Latin American milieu.

Some valid criticisms undoubtedly can and have been raised against IMF policies which, though recently showing signs of liberalization and flexible adjustment, still fail to do justice to the exasperating political and economic complexities of the task of curbing inflation in developing countries without stunting their growth. Those criticisms can be summarized as follows.

1. *The aggregative approach.* Until recently at least the absorbing preoccupation of the Fund's programs was the curbing of over-all excess demand, with but little effort to distinguish between consumption and investment expenditures, and to identify bottleneck sectors in which investment would have to be maintained, or even accelerated by an expansion, if needed, of foreign financing. The Fund's formalistic attitude of passing over the investment problem on the ground that its statutory function is confined to balance-of-payments problems is not helpful; in several cases, if stabilization programs are to be realistic, the Fund must take the initiative of coordinating with other investment agencies the provision of noninflationary financial resources for making short term correction of certain strategic bottlenecks; and offsetting unemployment effects arising from the contraction of nonpriority or inflated investment sectors.

2. *Underestimation of the effects of trade fluctuations.* The programming of foreign financial assistance in stabilization plans has often been made without reference to the vicissitudes of trade. Thus, through the deterioration of the terms of trade or the shrinkage of trade opportunities of the less-developed countries, the margin of foreign assistance originally designed to permit a certain level of imports may be completely nullified. The recent approval by the Fund of a scheme for compensatory financing of declines in export revenues (the so-called "fifth credit *tranche*") is a belated recognition of the problem but, from the viewpoint of the developing countries, the scheme fails to meet the requirements of *automaticity* and *additionality*. Thus, because the IMF maintains discretionary power to determine whether the decline in export receipts is due to circumstances beyond the country's control and whether the country concerned is properly cooperating with the Fund, the plan reintroduces, by the back door, the entire dispute on the technical correctness and political relevance of stabilization programs. Moreover, to the extent that the utilization of the fifth *tranche* merely substitutes for drawing out the ordinary credit *tranches,* access to which would become more stringent, there would be a purely illusory increase in the financial assistance to the developing countries.[13]

3. *The simultaneity of external and internal equilibrium.* The IMF pursues a fairly rigid policy of simultaneous execution of measures to correct the internal inflationary disequilibrium and to restore external balance. But the attainment of internal equilibrium is a difficult task at best, and requires minimization of the cost-push, an objective which is inconsistent with the rigid requirement of general devaluation or of immediate elimination of exchange-rate subsidies usually applicable to basic cost-of-living items. There is no denying that measures of the latter type are essential to correct internal and external imbalances but they do complicate the problem by superimposing on internal pressures the added cost-push of devaluation.[14] It may turn out to be realis-

---

[13] It must be noted, however, that by providing for compensation related directly to a shortfall in export receipts, irrespective of the behavior of capital inflows or service items, the scheme may in individual instances operate generously in favor of those developing countries whose losses of export revenues may have been offset by a favorable behavior of other balance-of-payments entries.

[14] On the basis of the recent experience of the Argentine and Chilean devaluations, Professor Harberger suggests that the inflationary cost-push arising from devaluations may have been underestimated in current discussion. "Certainly one must conclude . . . that devaluations can have very substantial effects on the level of prices—not only through their effects in raising income and in inducing the sub-

Economic Development and Inflation

tic in the future to recognize the need for a two-stage approach, the initial one limited to fiscal and monetary measures to check internal inflation, to be followed later by foreign-exchange measures designed to redress the external balance. This would of course presuppose acceptance on the part of the Fund of an increased balance-of-payments deficit during the first phase of stabilization programs.

4. *Underestimation of the political pitfalls of stabilization programs.* There appears to be also an underestimation of the political resistances generated by anti-inflationary programs applied to Latin American countries afflicted by chronic and acute inflation and distortions generated by the lag of certain strategic prices repressed through artificial price and exchange controls.

The major pitfalls in such stabilization programs can be thus described as follows: (a) During the initial phase of stabilization programs, there is frequently a sharp upsurge in the cost of living, due to the elimination of consumer subsidies, to exchange devaluation, and to decontrol of lagging prices (such as utility rates). Such *corrective inflation,* difficult for the man in the street to understand, tends to demoralize politically the stabilization effort at its very inception, particularly because those measures are likely to affect more painfully the low-income groups.[15] (b) Given the political rigidity of government expenditures, ceilings on credit to the private sector are more likely to be enforced than ceilings on government expenditure. Since the private sector accounts ordinarily for the major part of the supply of wage goods, such contraction of the private sector is likely to create additional supply rigidities, which have an inflationary effect. (c) One of the well-known inflationary distortions is excessive investment in inventories and scarcity of reserves for working capital. When credit ceilings are rapidly enforced a *cash crisis* may occur, because the businessmen are unable to monetize assets rapidly enough for the creation of

---

stitution of domestic for international goods." See "Some notes on inflation," paper submitted to the Rio de Janeiro Conference on Inflation and Growth, January, 1963. The inflationary effects of currency devaluation, however, may not be as serious as feared by Professor Harberger (a) if the previously subsidized exchange rates were financed through budget deficits, and (b) if the level of internal prices of international goods does not reflect the landed cost of imports because of the scarcity generated by exchange controls or quantitative restrictions on imports.

[15] For a thorough discussion of the mechanism of corrective inflation, see Simonsen, "A inflação no Brasil," pp. 216–219. The failure to understand this mechanism is at the root of the widespread objection on the part of Latin American economists to the use of indirect taxes as an anti-inflationary device.

working capital. Curtailment of production and unemployment may ensue, generating untoward supply effects and intolerable political resistance to the continuation of credit restraints. (d) Even when overall credit ceilings and controls are being imposed, *agricultural credit* should rate a high priority in view of its direct relevance to the supply of food; thus simultaneously with global credit restraints, a selective expansion should be permitted in agricultural credit, even if foreign resources have to be mobilized to provide a noninflationary source of financing.

Policy Conclusions: An Eclectic View

In the controversy between monetarists and structuralists, symbolized respectively by the IMF and ECLA, I place myself squarely in the middle, taking a rather eclectic view. My policy conclusions would then be as follows:

1. Traditional monetary controls, although undoubtedly an indispensable ingredient of stabilization plans, are of doubtful effectiveness if taken in isolation. If, for instance, the major burden is laid on control of bank credit, the following results may occur: (a) if the level of real wages is flexible, employment can be maintained but at the cost of declining real wages, a solution which is both socially unfair and politically unfeasible; (b) if the level of real wages is rigid, employment and output may have to be curtailed, thus aggravating both inflationary pressures and political resistance.

2. Fiscal policies must play a dominant role in stabilization programs. They should be aimed at compressing the consumption of high-income groups, as well as raising the marginal rate of taxation above the average rate by increasing the progressiveness of both excise and income taxes, by substituting *ad valorem* for specific charges, and by avoiding subsidization of the consumption of basic services through lagging utility and transportation rates.

3. Even though the unsatisfactory degree of national consensus in the socially nonintegrated societies in Latin America and the low level of public information on economic matters raise obstacles to the formulation and acceptance of "income policies," such as those that are increasingly the subject of public agreement in Western Europe and the United States, a constant attempt should be made to take into full account the political aspects of stabilization programs and to evolve publicly discussed guidance for the growth of incomes, in par-

Economic Development and Inflation 121

ticular of wages and salaries, in a way compatible with disinflationary objectives.[16]

4. The international financial assistance mobilized through the IMF and other agencies should be of a more flexible nature to take into account (a) the need to coordinate financial external support for stabilization measures with noninflationary financing for investments designed to alleviate bottleneck sectors; (b) the need to relate the planned level of foreign assistance to fluctuations in the export revenue of underdeveloped countries exposed to price instability; (c) the need for greater flexibility in the timing of internal stabilization measures and those designed for the correction of external imbalances, such as exchange-rate devaluation or withdrawal of subsidies on essential imports. The latter measures might well be dephased in time or, alternatively, the IMF might consider alleviating the immediate cost-push of devaluation by additional financial assistance designed to permit a temporary increase in the supply of imported goods.

5. In determining the level of foreign financial assistance needed for stabilization programs, attention should be given to the desirability of providing a noninflationary margin of external financing for selective credit expansion, in order to surmount the "working-capital crisis" of the transition to stabilization and to meet the need for additional stimulus to food production.

6. Special consideration should be given to orienting the import-substitution policy in the direction of manufactured goods that may have an export potential, so as to permit cost-reduction through economies of scale, and an increase of foreign-exchange availabilities for imports.

[16] For a discussion of "income policies" as a complement to monetary and fiscal measures in western Europe, see "Policies for Price Stability," report of the Working Party and Costs of Production and Prices by the OECD, December, 1962.

Some Notes on the History of the Alliance for Progress[1]

THE PAN AMERICAN MOVEMENT AND CONTINENTAL ECONOMIC COOPERATION

From Bolivar to the Eve of Operation Pan America

The Alliance for Progress, a political project imbued with libertarian idealism, sprang into being in 1961 within the framework of the Pan American movement.

It might be well to retrace the historical background of the Pan American organization. The Congress of Panama, in 1826, formalized the common aim of the new republics on the continent to defend their independence through inter-American cooperation. A few other meetings of little import were held prior to 1889 when, by initiative of the Secretary of State of the United States, James Blaine, the first Pan American Conference met in Washington and established in the capital of the United States of America a small business office which was later transformed into the Pan American Union.

The role played by the Monroe Doctrine in the development of inter-American relations has been frequently exaggerated. Monroism was formulated and applied originally as a unilateral gesture within the context of American foreign policy. Granting that it created a certain measure of protection (of merely partial usefulness) against European encroachments on the continent, it was only much later, under the Rio de Janeiro Treaty of 1947, that it was incorporated, in a way, into the inter-American system.

On the other hand, the participation by the United States in two

---

[1] "Some Notes on the History of the Alliance for Progress" is a heretofore unpublished essay.

extracontinental wars and the acquisition of political interests outside the continent, within the strategic picture of the cold war, imposed extreme limitations on the plausibility of the Doctrine.

The second Pan American Conference, held in Mexico in 1901, already saw Brazil appearing as a proponent of juridical formulas, a style which has characterized its behavior throughout the conferences held since then. At the third and fourth Conferences in 1908 (Rio de Janeiro) and 1910 (Buenos Aires), the interventions by the United States in various countries on the continent were bitterly criticized, without, however, there being any joint measure capable of debarring them. At the sixth Conference, held in Havana in 1928, the representatives of the United States devoted themselves extensively to explaining and defending such interventions.

Economic matters were brought into debate systematically for the first time in 1933, at the seventh Conference, in Montevideo, early during the administration of President Franklin Delano Roosevelt, which was beginning to face the problem of German commercial and economic infiltration in Latin America. Secretary of State Cordell Hull insistently argued at the time that it was necessary to lower inter-American tariffs so as to maintain for the United States a substantial market for manufactured products and for source of primary materials, then under grave threat. At the same time, the United States explicitly repudiated the "right to intervene."

Although the Chapultepec Conference, in 1945, made recommendations in favor of the "economic readjustment of the Hemisphere," it can be said that the emphasis on political negotiation and on the establishment of legal doctrine and instruments continued after 1945 and reached its climax in the Treaty of Rio de Janeiro, in 1947.

In 1948, in Bogota, the ninth Conference examined and approved, without great enthusiasm, a project for an Inter-American Economic Agreement. Economic development was already becoming a public and intense aspiration throughout the countries of Latin America. These countries encountered in the Marshall Plan, however, an obstacle to securing substantial resources from the United States, then primarily engaged in the reconstruction of Europe so as to deter the expansion of Communism.

Secretary Marshall's phrase "Between Europe in agony and a merely poor Latin America, we are compelled to give priority to Europe" summarized this conception, which has been called the *peninsular school,* due to the emphasis on economic aid as an "ideological bactericide" to be employed in the areas most exposed to Soviet pressure, particularly the European peninsula.

As President Felipe Herrera of the Inter-American Development Bank noted,

> ... the Marshall Plan rounds out a considerable volume of other resources which have flowed from the United States to Europe to aid recovery from the recent war. From the end of the war to mid-1951 the funds contributed by the United States for this purpose amount to 24 billion dollars, of which 10,300 million has been channeled through the Marshall Plan between the beginning of 1948 and June 30, 1951. As a whole, during a period of six years the flow of public resources from the United States to Europe had an average annual value of about 4 billion dollars.
>
> ... approximately 90% of the total funds distributed by the Marshall Plan were in the form of direct gifts, and only the remaining 10% were loans. In the case of Latin America, however, during the five-year period between 1957 and 1961, 70% of the aid from public funds came in the form of loans and only 30% in the form of gifts not requiring repayment.

In 1954, in Caracas, the theme of economic development again emerged and was given a livelier tone. At that meeting, Doctor Lleras Camargo, then secretary general of the Organization of American States, courageously diagnosed the inefficiency of the inter-American system. In Panama in 1956, President Eisenhower, hearkening to the mounting clamor from Latin America on the need for incrementing economic cooperation on the continent, promised a general overhaul of his country's foreign-aid policy. An Inter-American Committee of Presidential Representatives was established, which met several times, but whose recommendations had relatively little consequence.

In 1957 an Inter-American Economic Conference was held in Buenos Aires. Studies were made on the possibility of creating a common market in Latin America, on lines similar to that established in Europe. The conference also looked into the unfavorable effects of the European economic integration on the international trade of the underdeveloped countries of the Hemisphere. On that occasion the United States delegate, Mr. Robert Anderson, reaffirmed the position of his country that it would be unnecessary to create an inter-American bank, since an adequate number of international financing institutions already existed.

In May, 1958, Vice President Richard Nixon visited a number of countries in Latin America and was involved in the tumultuous episodes that led President Juscelino Kubitschek de Oliveira to write to President Eisenhower a letter proposing the launching of Operation Pan America.

Just prior to the launching of Operation Pan America, the inter-American system of economic cooperation was characterized by the following features: (a) an excessive emphasis on the political problems of inter-American relations, to the detriment of the primordial question of economic development; (b) the predominance of a formalistic tradition, abundantly expressed in legal and institutional constructions that obstructed the economico-social analysis of the needs for development and reform; (c) an incipient concern over the employment of the means for inter-American economic cooperation to combat economic underdevelopment; (d) the rising awareness, in the political and administrative leadership of the Latin American countries, that Latin America must be given a more active voice in the debate over world problems, including those of the cold war; (e) the realization, on the part of the United States government, that in its global anti-Communist strategy the Latin American problem should receive greater consideration than it had traditionally been given; and (f) a generalized resentment in Latin America against the residual treatment being accorded by the United States to its neighbors on the Hemisphere in its policy of foreign economic aid.

Operation Pan America

On July 20, 1958, in an address in Rio de Janeiro to the diplomatic representatives of the American countries, President Juscelino Kubitschek de Oliveira propounded the theses that Latin American should be accorded a more relevant participation in the treatment of international problems, and that underdevelopment was the fundamental question to the solution of which the resources of the inter-American system should be decisively applied.

On August 4, Secretary of State John Foster Dulles arrived in Brazil to discuss President Kubitschek's proposal, and on the 6th the Declaration of Brasília was published, the text of which, although only moderately voicing the enthusiasm and ambition of the Brazilian proposal, still represented in a way a commitment by the United States government in the statement that "the strengthening of American unity requires, among other measures, a dynamic effort to overcome the problems of underdevelopment . . . " and that this objective was "inseparable from the collective security of the Hemisphere."

Subsequently, the foreign ministers of the American republics met in Washington to discuss the necessary measures for the implementation of the Operation. It was decided to establish a special committee directly subordinated to the Council of the Organization of American States—the Committee of Twenty-One—for programming the execution of the new plan.

According to the Brazilian government, the main objectives of the Operation would be:

1. Definition of development as the achievement of a per capita revenue level that would make possible the inception of a cumulative and autonomous process of growth, with local resources, at a satisfactory rate, without sudden or grave institutional transformations;

2. The setting by agreement between the countries on the continent of such a target rate of growth of the gross product as would be required to keep up with population expansion and would facilitate the beginning of an autonomous process of development at a satisfactory rate;

3. Determination of the sources and amounts of public and private international funds that would be indispensable to supplement national resources;

4. Identification of the chief bottlenecks in the Latin American economies, to be removed by unilateral or by collective action—aiming primarily at increasing import capacity through expansion of international markets, at the establishment of an ample regional market, and at the creation of financial institutions for facilitating intraregional transactions, besides the expansion of industries intended to substitute for outside sources of supply;

5. Determination of the alternatives open to Latin America to ensure the growth rates adopted as targets for the Operation.

During the meetings of the Committee of Twenty-One in Washington in November and December, 1958, it became evident that there was opposition between the Brazilian attitude, ambitious and energetic in its adherence to the original concept of the Operation, and that of the United States, conservative and excessively cautious, tending to traditional, albeit possibly ampler, forms of economic cooperation, and rejecting, nevertheless, the basic objectives of global programming and quantification of targets.

On that occasion, the head of the Brazilian delegation, Ambassador

August Frederico Schmidt, reformulated the objectives of the conference in a specific manner, as follows:

1. The discussion of particular programs should be preceded by an agreement over the basic philosophy of the Operation, namely, the necessity of speeding up the economic development of Latin America.

2. As a working hypothesis, the Brazilian delegation suggested that a minimum income level be estimated, to be reached within a reasonable period, ranging between $400 and $500 per capita.

3. The items of the meeting's agenda should be examined in the light of these considerations.

Brazil's position was supported by a considerable Latin American majority, but it met with firm opposition on the part of the United States delegation, which feared committing its country implicitly to render economic assistance in accepting quantification of the objective and needs of Latin American development.

No substantial progress was achieved in subsequent meetings of the Committee of Twenty-One and of the various subcommittees, except the unification and consolidation of the Latin American viewpoint around the theses launched by Brazil.

The establishment, on April 8, 1959, of the Inter-American Bank for Economic Development was a concession on the part of United States policy and a victory for the Latin American countries. The evolution of the Cuban crisis, in the following year, appears to have contributed toward making evident the urgency of the problem of economic development. In July, 1960, in Newport, President Dwight Eisenhower stated his intention to propose a new and decisive program of economic assistance to the underdeveloped countries on the continent. From the so-called Eisenhower Plan evolved the $500 million Social Progress Trust Fund, authorized by the Congress of the United States on September 2, and now administered by the Inter-American Development Bank.

At the Bogota Conference in 1960 the Brazilian delegation defended vigorously the theses of the Operation, proclaiming the necessity of adopting a flexible program for economic cooperation that should permit, among other things, the complementation of investments in local currency, as well as the necessity of quantification of resources and of targets for Latin American development.

The Bogota Charter of that same year consolidated the gains of Operation Pan America, establishing that:

1. There should be instituted an inter-American development program for the purpose of executing measures to improve productivity

in the use of land, to raise living standards in rural areas, to expand housing facilities, to develop educational and training systems, to improve public health levels, and to increase the mobilization of domestic resources;

2. A special fund (Eisenhower Plan) would be created to be administered by the Inter-American Development Bank for the purpose of contributing capital and technical assistance to implement the above indicated measures;

3. The Latin American countries should reaffirm the necessity of obtaining additional resources for financing projects for basic industrial development.

On contrasting the benefits achieved through Operation Pan America by the end of 1960 with its original objectives as proposed by the government of Brazil, we can see that, despite the tenacity of the Brazilian effort and the support received from the majority of Latin American countries, those targets were not reached to any significant extent. The position taken by the United States government during the negotiations which culminated in the Bogota Conference was the important factor in this relative failure. That attitude was characterized by (a) a formalistic treatment of the suggestions and problems raised (as exemplified by the overcautious examination of these topics and by their sluggish circulation through the intricate institutional network of the OAS); (b) concessions on palliative tactical measures, of which those having major practical consequences were the support to the Inter-American Development Bank and the institution of the Social Progress Trust Fund; and (c) purely verbal concessions (generally welcomed by the Latin American countries) aiming at specification and concretization in an indeterminate and sometimes improbable future.

The principal gains of the Operation were the following:

1. The ruling classes in Latin America, and, in some countries, certain sectors of public opinion were made dramatically aware of the problem of economic underdevelopment and of the political alienation of the underdeveloped areas of the continent.

2. In the United States of America the governing classes became aware, if not of the necessity of contributing more substantially toward Latin American development, at least of the importance with which Latin American claims might become invested.

3. Objectively, the creation of the Inter-American Development Bank and of the Social Progress Trust Fund contributed in a modest

way toward enlarging the scarce sources of founds for financing economic development in Latin America.

THE ACT FOR INTERNATIONAL DEVELOPMENT

Principles and Criteria for Granting Foreign Aid

The provisions of the Act for International Development encompass a number of principles and criteria governing foreign aid. The main aims underlying the text of the Act can be summarized as follows:

1. To strengthen the economies of the underdeveloped friendly nations.

2. To encourage the flow of private investment capital:

It is the policy of the United States to strengthen friendly foreign countries by encouraging the development of their free economic institutions and productive capabilities, and by minimizing or eliminating barriers to the flow of private investment capital.[2]

3. To fulfill long-range objectives:

... it is the policy of the United States to make assistance available ... in scope and on a basis of an environment in which the energies of the peoples of the world can be devoted to constructive purposes, free of pressures and erosion by the adversaries of freedom.[3]

4. To serve as an instrument in the strategy of the cold war:

Also the Congress reaffirms its conviction that the peace of the world and the security of the United States are endangered as long as international Communism continues to attempt to bring under Communist domination peoples now free and independent and to keep under domination peoples once free but now subject to such domination. It is therefore the policy of the United States to continue to make available to other free countries and peoples, upon request, assistance of such nature and in such amounts as the United States deems advisable and as may be effectively used by free countries and peoples to help them maintain their freedom.[4]

5. To stimulate growth and favor the equilibrium of the economy of the United States:

It is the sense of this Congress that assistance under this Act should be complemented by the furnishing under any other Act of surplus agricultural commodities and by disposal of excess property under this and other Acts.[5]

[2] AID, 1961, section 102.
[3] *Ibid.*   [4] *Ibid.*   [5] *Ibid.*

In enunciating the criteria for the granting of loans for development, the Act stipulates that consideration should be given, among other matters, to "the possible effects upon the United States economy, with special reference to areas of substantial labor surplus, of the loan involved."[6]

6. To associate the other industrialized Western countries, as well as international organizations, with the effort for development financing:

It is the sense of Congress that, where feasible, the United States Government invite friendly nations to join in missions to consult with countries which are recipients of assistance under this part on the possibilities for joint action to assure the effective development of plans for the economic development of such recipient countries and the effective use of assistance provided them; and that the President may request the assistance of international financial institutions in bringing about the establishment of such missions.

The criteria could be summarized in the following manner:

1. Assistance is to be based on solid long-range plans.

2. It must benefit the people of the recipient country socially and economically.

3. It is to be granted to countries having the resources and the will to engage themselves in a program for economic development:

Assistance shall be based upon sound plans and programs; be directed toward the social as well as the economic aspects of economic development; be responsive to the efforts of the recipient countries to mobilize their own resources and help themselves; be cognizant of the external and internal pressures which hamper their growth; and should emphasize long range development planning as the primary instrument of such growth.

4. Countries having lower potentialities for development should receive technical assistance on a priority basis:

In countries and areas which are in the earlier stages of economic development, programs of development of education and human resources through such means as technical cooperation shall be emphasized . . .[7]

5. In countries having a predominantly agrarian economy, preference is to be given to programs of community development, domestic "cottage" industries, improvement of agricultural technique, and local self-help programs:

[6] *Ibid.*, section 202b.
[7] *Ibid.*, section 211b.

The History of the Alliance for Progress

... [in countries having a predominantly agrarian economy] emphasis shall be placed on programs which reach the people in such a country, who are engaged in agrarian pursuits or who live in the villages or rural areas in such a country, including programs which will assist them in the establishment of indigenous cottage industries, in the improvement of agricultural methods and techniques, and which will encourage the development of local programs of self-help and mutual cooperation.[8]

In such countries emphasis shall be placed also upon programs of community development which will promote stable and responsible governmental institutions at the local level.[9]

Critical Observations

Inadequacies of the Criteria Governing the Granting of Foreign Aid

The first critical observation generally made on the criteria for the granting of foreign aid deals with the lack of a realistic viewpoint for evaluation of the problem of underdevelopment. The prerequisites provided by the current legislation for the granting of foreign aid for development are conditions that normally could apply adequately only in the case of developed countries.

Assistance shall be based upon sound plans and programs; be directed toward the social as well as the economic aspects of economic development; be responsive to the efforts of the recipient countries to mobilize their own resources and help themselves; be cognizant of the external and internal pressures which hamper their growth; and should emphasize long range development planning as the primary instrument of such growth.

In the second place, although the legislation affirms that it is a responsibility of the United States "to help to make an historic demonstration that the economic growth and political democracy can go hand in hand," in the practical evaluation of the performances of the countries, for the effect of the economic aid, this principle is not given adequate priority. Often performance is analyzed with an exaggerated emphasis on financial behavior, neglecting other factors, such as the maintenance of democratic procedures, the degree of social mobility, the speed of incorporation of the masses into the political process. These factors, though making it more difficult to maintain financial discipline, are better measurements of the long-run economic and so-

[8] *Ibid.*, section 461.
[9] *Ibid.*, section 110.

cial viability. Even within the economic and financial sphere there is often a "stability bias" which leads to easier acceptance of situations of stability without growth than of growth with inflation.

In the third place, it should be pointed out that, in spite of the provisions of section 202 of the Act for International Development, authorizing appropriations of $1.5 million over a period of four years subsequent to 1962, the mass of resources intended for economic aid is voted annually. There is always, therefore, an element of insecurity which impairs the planning capacity both of the Agency and of the recipient countries.

On the other hand, this imprevisibility acts as a negative stimulus in regard to the achievement, by the governments of the recipient countries, of the reforms that are indispensable for their economic development. Many of these governments do not feel disposed to face the political wear and tear which reforms involve, unless they are assured of a regular flow of external resources which might permit them, within a relatively short run, to achieve economic results that are visible and, therefore, susceptible of political utilization.

Finally, one basic criticism transcends the limits of the Agency itself. Comments have been made elsewhere on the tendency of United States public opinion and of some sectors of the Administration to sacrifice sociologic intelligence in favor of a moralistic viewpoint in the evaluaton of the phenomenon of underdevelopment. This viewpoint focuses preferentially on the degree of perfection in the discharge of imagined tasks, imposed *a priori,* and omits from its horizon the politico-social complexity of the underdeveloped world. Hence the emphasis on the criteria of "self-help" and the insistence on "solid programming," in conjunction with an overlight appreciation of the democratic integrity of the regimes of the underdeveloped countries and their rate of economic growth.

Administrative Intricacy

One of the most frequent criticisms made about the Agency for International Development bears on the operational complexity of its bureaucracy and, consequently, on its slowness in reaching decisions. Our experience shows that it takes from eight months to a year and a half to secure approval of a project.

Naturally, this dilatoriness causes all sorts of inconveniences; and, among other things, it serves as an obstacle to the "sound and effective

The History of the Alliance for Progress

long-range planning" of underdeveloped countries that are, because of their own conditions, characteristically lacking in external sources of financing. As may be imagined, it is very difficult for an underdeveloped country to stay within the lines of a long-range plan, when it cannot count on rapid decisions concerning certain sectors of its planning. An integrated plan presupposes the interlinking of various sectorial plans and, necessarily, a scheduling of target dates that cannot be done arbitrarily.

In order to better illustrate the complexity of AID bureaucracy, it might be interesting to review the stages through which a development-aid loan project has to pass on the way to approval:

1. The project is submitted to the AID Mission in the applicant county.

2. The local AID Mission examines the project in the light of a system of targets and priorities. Once it is found that the project fulfills the conditions prescribed for AID help in the recipient country, the Mission and the local government together go over the plans of the latter relating to the activity in question.

3. After a preliminary request is made by the government of the country, the project is forwarded to the Regional Office of AID, with a recommendation.

4. A "project officer" is assigned to make a preliminary examination, in which his first task is to find out if there are other available sources of financing. Among other steps, he has to take the project to the AID-EXIMBANK Coordinating Commission to ascertain if the Bank is disposed to finance it. The project will continue with AID only if the decision in the case is negative.

5. In the next stage, the "project officer" prepares a preliminary report and forwards the project to the Assistant Administrator in charge of the Regional Office. If the latter finds that the project merits consideration, he authorizes a thorough examination.

6. The Assistant Administrator appoints a working group of specialists to conduct the aforementioned examination and to send the project through a number of organs and committees, depending on its nature.

7. Next, it is submitted to the Committee on Loans for Development (this requirement does not apply to projects valued at less than $2 million).

8. It is forwarded to the National Consultative Committee on International Financial and Monetary Affairs.

9. On the basis of the decisions of the two foregoing committees, the Administrator approves or rejects the project.

10. After approval by the Administrator, the interested party is notified that the loan has been granted, and informed of the conditions that said party must fulfill in order to receive it.

11. On acceptance of the conditions, the loan agreement is prepared, negotiated, and concluded.

Administrative Instability

The direction of AID is held to be one of the most ungrateful tasks in the American Administration. Within the last two years of the American experiment in foreign aid, it went from James Riddleberger (1959–1961), to Henry Labouisse (1961), to Fowler Hamilton (1961–1962), and finally to David Bell.

This administrative instability reflects in part the extremely low prestige of the Agency in public opinion and in the Congress. From the viewpoint of public opinion, the idea of foreign aid is associated with prodigality in the use of the taxpayers' money either to swell conspicuous consumption by corrupt foreign elites or to support governments that show little loyalty to the Western cause.

The gravest effect of this administrative instability is the instability of criteria which accompanies it. Indeed, each new administrator is forced to meditate upon the failure of his predecessor and to search for new criteria that may provide the Agency with a better reception by the people and by Congress and, consequently, with more generous funds with which to increase the efficiency of its action.

By the circumstances of its origin, AID is the result of the amalgamation of two agencies—the Development Loan Fund and the Economic Cooperation Administration—which already had certain operational traditions. Mr. Frank Coffin, commenting upon the fusion of the two agencies, classified it as "complicated chemistry." Actually, it was not only necessary to readapt the two agencies to work under a unified leadership, but also to adapt them to a geographic operational system, when their traditional systems of operation had been functional in nature.

THEORIES OF FOREIGN AID

Hans Morgenthau—A Political Theory of Foreign Aid

Mr. Hans Morgenthau, in an article published in the *American Political Science Review* of June, 1962, tries to create what he calls "an intelligible theory of foreign aid." His position reflects a line of thought that is quite widespread in public opinion and even among some circles in the Administration and in Congress.

The basis for this reasoning is that the foreign-aid effort does not produce compensative political effects and may even bring negative results in time. Furthermore, along the same line of thought, the major part of aid intended for underdeveloped countries is supposedly channelled for the benefit of corrupt and incompetent hegemonic groups and never reaches the majority of the people of a recipient nation. Consequently, it is of urgent necessity to apply criteria capable of turning foreign aid into an efficient tool of American political strategy; the urgency is all the more evident by reason of the competition from the Sino-Soviet bloc, whose criteria of foreign aid are supposedly more realistic and efficient in terms of political effect.

In short, what is proposed by Morgenthau and by others who, with greater or lesser sophistication, think like him, is to drain the foreign-aid concept of all ideological content, turning it into a cold and efficient instrument of political action.

There is, at the root of this type of ratiocination, an element of moral recrimination against countries which have been unable to organize themselves for the solution of their own problems and which are, on the other hand, potentially capable of subjecting themselves to the Sino-Soviet influence, so that foreign aid granted them may become a bad investment both politically and economically. It might be said that this thesis has an isolationist component that seeks to reduce the intensity of American action in the foreign-aid sector, trying to keep it to the minimum demanded by the strategy of the cold war.

In order to make possible the establishment of a coherent policy designed to provide guidance for the programs of foreign aid, Mr. Morgenthau sets out six types of programs, classified according to their purposes:

1. *Humanitarian assistance.* Such aid aims at supplying relief to populations victimized by cataclysms—floods or earthquakes, for instance. This aid has no direct political objectives, although it may create conditions facilitating political action.

2. *Aid for subsistence.* This type of aid is designed to fill budgetary needs of governments (such as those of Jordan and Nigeria) that do not have resources at their disposal for the maintenance of a minimum standard of public services. It aims, in the final analysis, at preventing political chaos and maintaining the status quo, although without in-

creasing the viability of the beneficiary governments. Aid for subsistence loses efficiency whenever the recipient government is confronted by considerable political opposition.

3. *Assistance for bribery.* After a brief historical review of the evolution of bribery, Morgenthau suggests that foreign aid serves today, in many cases, as a mask for bribery. However, the replacement of the traditional bribe, "a relatively straightforward transaction," by the sophisticated modern form in which it is presented as economic aid, tends to bring trouble both for the grantor and for the recipient: the former does not obtain the political effects primarily desired, while the latter does not achieve the ostensibly declared economic results.

4. *Military aid.* This is the traditional type of foreign aid in any system of alliance. At the present time, Morgenthau notes, it serves to mask other types of aid. Military aid to Yugoslavia, for instance, would be masked bribery. The delivery of jet planes to underdeveloped countries serves to impart prestige to the recipient government rather than to achieve proper military purposes. Finally, economic aid is granted under the disguise of military assistance, because of the reluctance of the Congress to "vote important sums for economic aid, in opposition to its readiness to vote practically any amount for military purposes."

5. *Aid for prestige.* Such aid is granted to governments engaged in projects of "conspicuous industrialization," that is, projects that function as symbols of progress although they do not correspond to the economic necessities of the country.

6. *Aid for economic development.* In analyzing the problem of foreign aid for development, Mr. Morgenthau points out four correlations, generally held as true, but whose validity he seeks to deny. The first correlation is that between injection of capital and technology and economic development. Mr. Morgenthau calls attention to physical, social, and human limitations of certain countries, that would render them inaccessible to the process of economic development. "To put it bluntly," said he, "as there are bums and beggars, so there are bum and beggar nations. They may be recipients of charity, but short of a miraculous transformation of their collective intelligence and character, what they receive from the outside is not likely to be used for economic development."

Mr. Morgenthau goes on to argue that economic interests exist in the underdeveloped countries that prevent resources destined for economic development from being applied for that purpose. The hegemonic groups in several of these countries are interested in the maintenance

The History of the Alliance for Progress

of the status quo. Thus, foreign aid "is more likely to accentuate unsolved political and social problems than to bring them closer to solution." For this reason, in order that aid be efficient it is indispensable that, parallel to its granting, there be made political reforms or economic reforms with political consequences, the "promotion of drastic social changes . . . although it may create conditions for an uncontrollable revolution" which can generate political consequences unfavorable to the United States.

The third "false correlation" would be that between aid for economic development and the development of democratic institutions. The most probable hypothesis, argues Morgenthau, is that the moral and intellectual prerequisites that are essential to economic development will not be distributed throughout the nation but rather that they will be concentrated within a small minority. Therefore, release of the process depends on the imposition of the will of a minority over the will of the nation as a whole.

Finally, he refers to the inexistence of a relationship between economic development and a peaceful foreign policy, and recalls the example of the Soviet Union which could engage in an expansionist foreign policy only after it had overcome the barrier of underdevelopment.

In concluding, Mr. Morgenthau reasons as follows: foreign aid will be "efficient" only to the extent of the possibility of identifying concrete situations with the categories described and of granting aid that is adequate for the purpose aimed at, subject to criteria governing the global foreign policy of the grantor country.

A clear evaluation should also be made of the consequences of the simultaneous granting of several types of aid. Thus, bribes given to the hegemonic group, as well as aid for prestige and aid for subsistence, tend to strengthen the political and economic status quo of the recipient country; military aid will tend to influence the structure of political power and may have economic consequences such as aggravation of inflationary pressure; economic aid, on the contrary, will tend to provoke modifications in the status quo and, consequently, it may annul the effects aimed at by other types of aid.

It is especially difficult to obtain coexistence between programs of aid for prestige and those for economic development.

Afghanistan is the classical example of this dilemma. The Soviet Union, by paving the streets of Kabul, chose a kind of prestige aid that is irrelevant to economic development. The United States, by building a hydroelectric dam in a remote part of the country, chose economic development, the very existence of which is unknown to most Afghans and the benefits of which will not appear for years to come.

The example given aims at emphasizing the importance of the effect of aid on the prestige of the grantor nation. In this sense, argues Morgenthau, aid for economic development bringing immediate results is a more efficient political instrument than aid for projects having slow economic maturity. It is equally important to establish unequivocally the relationship between the aid and the country that gives it. Finally, it is necessary to correlate the general policy of the grantor country with the aid extended by it, so as to create a favorable image of the grantor in the recipient country.

In short, "a policy of foreign aid is no different from the diplomatic, or military policy of propaganda. They are all weapons in the political armory of the nation."

Selective Criteria

There is a tendency in the American Administration to establish criteria channeling economic aid toward areas and sectors selected under prioritarian and therefore discriminatory points of view.

Mr. Fowler Hamilton, then administrator of the Agency for International Development, on announcing the Plan for Long Range Strategy (to be discussed later in this study) in November, 1963, stated that the idea of the new plan was to establish "what each dollar used in foreign aid can buy for the American people," and that the desired effect of maximizing the returns from foreign aid would be obtained by "placing more eggs in fewer baskets, so that the foreign aid effort be more dramatically visible."

The following is a summary of two documents which are representative of this tendency.

Chester Bowles' Criteria

Mr. Chester Bowles, advisor to President Kennedy on problems of underdeveloped countries, presented a memorandum in August, 1963, suggesting specific criteria for the programming of economic aid. It is his belief that the operational criteria for distribution of foreign aid should be directly inspired by the principles established in the 1961 Act for International Development. Curtailment of such principles

The History of the Alliance for Progress

could be justified only by reason of imperative contingencies of the cold war. Even so, when the dominating criterion was a political one, precise terms of reference should be established that would permit a measure of objectivity and coherence of judgment.

The five basic principles established by the Act for International Development, 1961, are the following:

1. Foreign aid should aim at creating or strengthening independent nations, capable of making their own decisions.

The Congress declares it to be a primary necessity, opportunity and responsibility of the United States, and consistent with its traditions and ideals . . . to help make a historic demonstration that political democracy can produce an enlarged community of free, stable and self-reliant countries and reduce world tensions and insecurity.

2. Aid must suppose the existence of a realistic national plan lining up all available factors with a view to a balanced economic and social growth.

Assistance will be based upon sound plans and programs, be directed towards the social as well as the economic aspects of economic development; be responsible to the efforts of the recipient countries to mobilize their own resources and help themselves; . . . should emphasize long range development assistance as the primary instrument of such growth.

3. High priority should be given to plans to provide better economic and social conditions for the rural populations which constitute 75 percent of the total population of the underdeveloped world.

Whenever the President determines that the economy of any country is in major part an agrarian economy, emphasis shall be placed on programs which reach the people in such country who are engaged in agrarian pursuits or who live in the villages or rural areas.

4. Aid is to be concentrated on countries possessing the skill and will to achieve speedy integrated political and economic growth.

On the basis of such principles, Mr. Bowles suggests the necessity of classifying the nations which desire to benefit from American aid, in accordance with their economic needs, capabilities, and desire for development. To this end he proposes the following questions, the answers to which would permit the establishment of priorities for the granting of foreign aid:

1. Is the per capita income level of the country sufficient to ensure a

minimum standard of living and an adequate rate of savings and investment, in case the revenue is distributed evenly?

2. Is the government of the country competent and capable of maintaining internal order and of promoting an integrated program of economic and social development?

3. Does the government possess a plan for long-range development which envisages a realistic combination of domestic resources and foreign aid?

4. Is its tax system socially equitable? Is its fiscal administration good? Are its fiscal revenues sufficient to ensure the financing, in local currency, of its necessities?

5. Is the public administration relatively efficient and honest?

6. What is the percentage of rural population in the composition of the country's total population?

7. Is there a fair distribution of land, or are there plans to improve such distribution?

8. Are there any realistic plans under execution to improve conditions of health, education, and housing both in the urban and rural areas?

9. Can the government (whatever be its political nature) rely on sufficient support from public opinion to permit it to achieve a bold program of social and economic development?

10. Are there in existence favorable political conditions for domestic and foreign private investment?

11. Does the government maintain a real control over expenditures of foreign-exchange availabilities on subjects of a sumptuary nature? Are their indications of a real effort being made to prevent migration of domestic capital to foreign countries?

The answer to these questions would permit classification of countries into four categories calling for differential treatment from the viewpoint of foreign aid.

First category: Countries whose difficulties result primarily from bad utilization of existing resources

In this category would be included countries with a per capita GNP substantially above $350, such as Greece, Venezuela, Lebanon, Cyprus, Singapore, Chile, Panama, Uruguay, Jamaica, Trinidad, and Argentina. Aid would be granted only if they were disposed to adopt measures—such as tax reform, agrarian reform, discipline in the use of foreign-exchange availabilities—tending to correct socioeconomic vices. Aid to those countries would be temporary and stop-gap in nature. Only the contingencies of the cold war would justify continuation of aid to the countries not disposed to effect the salutary reforms.

Second category: Countries with GNP insufficient for autonomous development, but which show capability and the will to carry out programs for social progress and speedy economic growth

The countries to be included in this category would be those with a per capita GNP under $350. They would receive priority treatment. One suggested measure for helping such countries is to have Congress authorize five-year aid plans, so as to increase efficiency of application of the resources furnished.

Whenever possible, encouragement would be given to the creation of "consortiums" into whose makeup would go resources from United States aid, from international financial organizations, and from other industrialized countries of the West.

The aid extended to these countries (India, Pakistan, Formosa, San Salvador, Colombia, Tunisia, and Nigeria were among those cited) would be de-bureaucratized and substantial, so as to serve as "dramatic showcase examples of what outstanding performance by a recipient nation backed by generous U.S. assistance can accomplish."

Third category: Countries whose GNP is insufficient for autonomous development, and which do not present the same positive qualities of will and capability featuring the countries in the second category

For the countries included in this category, aid should be concentrated on sectors whose performance is satisfactory. In no way should aid be granted that could bring on aggravation of economic and social injustice. The following criteria should be taken into consideration in granting aid to such countries: (a) the country's initial stage of development; (b) the political risk faced by the government in achieving reform; and (c) the achievements of other countries on a similar level of development. Aid could be granted for the purpose of encouraging certain reforms that would permit the upgrading of such countries to the priority category.

Fourth category: Countries whose GNP is absolutely insufficient for the developmental take-off and which lack competence and organiza-

tion for the adequate utilization of credit for development or budgetary purposes

Aid would be granted with a view to the formation of technical and administrative staffs and for humanitarian purposes.

The "Long-Range Assistance Strategy" (LAS)

Last November Mr. Frank Coffin, deputy administrator of the Agency for International Development, announced a plan for Long-Range Assistance Strategy which was to be applied in its initial stage to about twelve countries, selected in accordance with the criteria indicated: (a) the importance of the country from the viewpoint of United States foreign policy; (b) the importance of American aid to the country's developmental process; (c) the degree of political stability; (d) the economic policy adopted by the country, with evaluation of the emphasis placed on its social and economic development toward ensuring good prospects of effective development; (e) the existence of a reasonably well-worked-out plan or program for national development; and (f) the availability of reliable statistical information.

The countries to benefit under the new plan were to be selected shortly, in order that the assistance programs be included in the AID budget for the 1964 fiscal year. It was reported that the following countries were chosen for the first stage of the experiment: India, Pakistan, Colombia, Nigeria, Formosa, Thailand, Sudan, Tunisia, Turkey, and Iran.

According to all indications, the predominating criterion will be political. All the countries expected to be included in the first phase of LAS are either directly on the active frontiers of the cold war or near them, and not all could be selected if the predominating criterion were an economic one.

The M.I.T. Approach

In 1960, a group of professors of the Massachusetts Institute of Technology submitted to the Foreign Relations Committee of the Senate a report *(Economic, Social and Political Change in the Underdeveloped Countries and its Implications for United States Policy)* intended as a critical inventory of the conceptual framing of United States foreign-assistance programs.

This report was later enlarged and published under the title of *The*

Emerging Nations. The coordination of the work was conducted by Professors Max Millikan and Donald Blackmer and among its collaborators were Professors Walt Rostow and Paul Rosenstein-Rodan.

The report presents a broad and sophisticated version of the foreign-aid problem. Many of the authors who collaborated in it occupy, or have occupied, important positions in the Administration and were instrumental in setting up the principles of the Act for International Development in 1961, which reformulated the United States position in regard to economic assistance to underdeveloped countries.

Professor Rostow was an advisor to the late President Kennedy and is chairman of the Council on Policy and Planning; Professor Paul N. Rosenstein-Rodan is one of the "Nine Wise Men" of the OEA; Professor Max Millikan was head of the work group for the re-evaluation of the Foreign Assistance Act. The document thus acquires a special significance, since it contains the theoretical thought of a number of persons capable of exercising concrete influence over the Administration's political decisions.

In their analysis of United States interest in the "transitional process" (modernization of traditional societies), the authors point out the following objectives: (a) that the new country be capable of maintaining its independence, especially vis-à-vis powers that are hostile to the United States; (b) that such country does not resort to violence in its international relations; (c) that it be capable of maintaining an organized and solid government, disposed to abstain from totalitarian controls; (d) that it accept the principles of an open society and that it be disposed to accept international measures for economic, political, and social control.

Of the four objectives indicated, there are two—abstention from totalitarian controls and acceptance of the principles of an open society—that are generally omitted or minimized by the foreign-aid administrators even though special emphasis was placed on them by legislative act.

Further on, in focusing on the problem of loans for development, the report indicated the following criteria:

1. Economic criteria guiding foreign assistance must be firmly applied and clearly expressed. Such criteria would serve as stimuli to the governments of the recipient countries to enact reforms and adaptations necessary to the process of development.

2. Aid for development must be on a long-range basis. It is necessary that, once the economic criteria are fulfilled, the recipient country

be assured of continued aid which would permit a solid and efficient programming for allocation of foreign resources in its development program.

3. The capital offered should be adequate in quantity and the conditions under which it is offered should be flexible.

According to the authors' estimate, United States assistance for purposes of economic development should be increased by U.S. $1 billion yearly in the next five years. This would mean that economic aid would correspond to 0.6 percent of the U.S. Gross National Product. This aid could be reduced slightly in the next five-year period, and thenceforth reduced substantially in measure with the speeding-up of the process of domestic capital formation in the underdeveloped countries.

The amount of aid is an essential element for stimulation to the recipient governments so that they become disposed to enact reforms which, at short range, may tend to provoke political attrition.

4. It is necessary that the loans be channelled to all the main sectors of the economy, in order to preclude the formation of bottlenecks with negative economic and psychological consequences.

5. The preparation of national development plans should be encouraged.

6. Collaboration between the underdeveloped countries and international financing organizations should be encouraged, in order to eliminate or diminish the participation of bilateral assistance in the total resources received from abroad.

The authors classify the countries into three groups for the purposes of granting foreign assistance:

1. *Neotraditional societies.* Societies which are close to the traditional stage, where only a minority has been exposed to contacts with the modern world. This category includes nearly all of Negro Africa, several countries of the Middle East, some areas in Asia and Latin America. The aid effort should be centered upon the formation of human resources and the principal instrument of aid should be technical assistance.

2. *Transitional societies.* Societies which have already embarked on a process of modernization—such as Pakistan, Iran, Iraq, Burma—where a relatively modern urban sector coexists with a traditionalistic rural sector. The greater part of these societies face problems resulting from the circumstance of their having structures which belong to a modern political and social system, but which do not function adequately.

United States policy should press the governments of these countries to improve the efficiency of their bureaucracies. Most countries in this category possess a defective distribution of land ownership. Agrarian reform, accompanied by supplementary measures—agricultural credit and technical assistance, for instance—should be encouraged. Finally, on termination of this initial phase, which is essential in order that private entrepreneurs and the government become aware of the national reality in their countries, attention might be given to a concentrated plan of assistance for development.

3. *Actively modernizing societies.* Countries, such as India, Brazil, the Philippines, and Taiwan, which have already attained a third stage in the modernization process and are prepared for the stage of autonomous growth. These countries possess governments which are relatively stable; they have made considerable progress in social development and regimentation of human resources; they are capable of a realistic insight which permits them to deal, simultaneously and in a realistic way, with the problems confronting the main sectors of their economies.

The primary task to be carried out in such cases is the mobilizing of a large quantity of resources for development. The countries in this category should formulate long-range programs instituting targets both for the public sector and for the private sector of their economies. They should be able to count upon commitments for a flow of foreign aid during a period of several years.

In any event, "the basic objective of United States economic policy, in the latter stages of development, should be that of ensuring that the advance toward the stage of autonomous growth is not impaired by a lack of foreign currency availabilities."

Finally, the authors emphasize the necessity of creating necessary stimuli for the processing of "democratic development," so that an "open society with a creative people" be developed in those countries.

The Alliance for Progress

Objectives and Means

On May 31, 1961, in an address from the White House, President John F. Kennedy announced a new and far-reaching program of economic cooperation with Latin America, a program whose general lines he had already mentioned during his campaign. The main points of the Alliance for Progress were as follows:

1. The effort should be made in a decisive way by the American nations to mobilize their resources and modify their social standards in order that everyone, and not just a privileged minority, should be benefited. As a counterpart to the Latin American national efforts, the United States would furnish resources having sufficient magnitude and range to reach the goals to be established.

2. The Inter-American Economic and Social Council (IAECOSOC) would meet shortly, at ministerial level, to initiate the broad planning that would constitute the foundations of the Alliance. Each Latin American country should formulate its own plan for long-range development, providing for priority targets, standards of monetary stability, machinery for executing the social reforms, stimulation of private initiative and activity, and application of the maximum national effort. These plans would constitute the basis for distribution of external resources.

3. Support would be given to all regional economic integration concurrent toward the establishment of broader markets and greater opportunities for competition.

4. The United States would cooperate in the study of problems of the market in primary products, seeking practicable methods to overcome the harmful features of that market.

5. The United States would intensify immediately the Food-for-Peace emergency program.

6. The programs of technical assistance and cultural cooperation would be expanded.

In a way, 1961 was repeating the situation in 1933, when a Democratic Administration, impelled by external circumstances and in the aftermath of an electoral campaign, opened a new outlook for the Latin American policy of the United States. In 1933 the "Big Stick" was eschewed in favor of the "Good Neighbor Policy" in response to the need for economic and political cooperation with Latin America. In 1961 the theme launched by Brazil in Operation Pan America was basically accepted by the United States, not as a tactical and attenuated reaction such as had occurred under the Eisenhower Administration, but rather as an innovating vision of the problems of the Hemisphere.

There followed the Punta del Este Conference, in August, 1961, when the commitment was itemized and codified. Basically, the Charter of Punta del Este established the following objectives to be achieved in Latin America within a decade, through the economic and technical cooperation of the American countries: (a) an autonomous and cumulative growth rate of 2.5 percent yearly per capita, with a reasonable regional and social distribution, as a symptom of a balanced and diversified expansion of agriculture and industry; (b) the elimination of adult illiteracy and the achievement of a minimum of six years of schooling, beside the general elevation of quality and adequacy of the educational systems; (c) a raise of five years in life expectancy, through a number of sanitary and social measures, including the supply of potable water and construction of sewer systems for 75 percent of the urban and 50 percent of the rural population; (d) the construction of a sufficient number of homes to expedite a solution of the housing problem; (e) the stabilization of the prices of import and export products and increase in the foreign currency revenues of the Latin American countries; (f) the stabilization of internal prices in those countries; and (g) a strengthening of the movements toward regional economic integration.

Secretary of the Treasury Douglas Dillon made this pertinent evaluation of the Alliance:

We welcome the revolution of rising expectations among our peoples and we intend to transform it into a revolution of rising satisfactions. To carry out these principles will often require difficult and far-reaching changes. It will require a strengthening of tax systems so that would-be evaders will know they face strict penalties, and so that taxes are assessed in accordance with ability to pay. It will require land reform so that under-utilized soil is put to full use and so that farmers can own their own land. It will require lower interest rates on loans to small farmers and small business. It will require greatly increased programs of education, housing and health. And for the United States it will require a clear acceptance of further responsibilities to aid our sister republics . . . Future development loans made by our new aid agency will be on a long-term basis running . . . up to 50 years. We also intend to make the bulk of these loans at low or zero rates of interest. Looking to the years ahead, and to all sources of external financing—from international institutions, from Europe and Japan as well as from North America, from new private investment as well as from public funds—Latin America, if it takes the necessary internal measures, can reasonably expect its own efforts to be matched by an inflow of capital during the next decade amounting to at least $20 billion. And most of this will come from public sources. The problem . . . will no longer lie in shortages of external capital, but in organizing effective development programs so that both domestic and foreign capital can be put to work rapidly, wisely and well . . . It is especially urgent to set up a task force on land reform . . . Enlarged expenditures for economic and social progress call for the reduction of . . . military expenditures ... The development of measures to stabilize, strengthen and enlarge the markets for Latin American exports must ... be an integral part of the Alliance for Progress. The United States is ready to cooperate in seeking workable solutions for commodity problems.

It was agreed that the implementation of the Alliance was to be a duty of existing national and inter-American agencies. The Organization of American States would be charged with the main responsibility for execution of the program. The idea of a high-level guiding commission, with broad responsibilities, was vigorously supported by the United States in company with the smaller countries but was objected to by the larger Latin American countries, including Brazil and particularly Argentina, on the grounds that such an institution would have three main drawbacks: a limitation of national sovereignty; the risk of standardizing economic and social planning on improperly generic terms; and excessive restriction of the area of bilateral financial negotiation. This latter position prevailed in the end, and the newly created Committee of Nine was given a merely supervisory and consultative function.

At the present time, there seems to be a tendency to return to the idea of a Committee of Nine with a considerably broader capacity, enabling it even to participate directly in the placement of available resources for the development of Latin America. The São Paulo ministerial meeting of the Inter-American Economic and Social Council, in November, 1963, decided to set up an Inter-American Coordinating Committee for the Alliance for Progress (CIAP) with much broader functions than those assigned to the Committee of Nine.

Critique of the Alliance

The First Year

During its first year the Alliance for Progress did not produce outstanding results, the consensus in Latin America and within a considerable portion of American public opinion being that the program presents substantial deficiencies in conception and especially in instrumentation.

On the other hand, the economic and social development of Latin America continues to proceed at an insufficient rate. At the Mexico City meeting, in October, 1963, of the Inter-American Economic and Social Council, this fact was verified officially. In the cautious words of one of the documents of the Conference, "the rate of economic growth in Latin America has improved only modestly and is still below the long-term objectives of the Alliance."

The United States government has likewise recognized, albeit in temperate terms, the difficulties of the Alliance and the fact that the major part of Latin America is in "relative stagnation," as was declared at the Mexico Conference. A high official of the U.S. State Department, Mr. Michael Blumenthal, said recently that "the Latin American economic picture is not as bright as we would like to see it. Production in the area, which expanded 7% in 1957, slowed to about 4% in 1961, while population increased by close to 3% during 1961. Last year, therefore, per capita increase in GNP was only about 1%. The picture for 1962 appears to be no brighter."

There are two distinct problems here, that must be considered separately:

1. *The deficiencies of the Alliance.* These deficiencies can be measured objectively (a) by the abatement in the flow of public and private capital into Latin America; (b) by the slow rhythm of implementation of structural reforms and of planning; (c) by the continued deterioration in the terms of trade; (d) subjectively, by the meager support from the press, public opinion, and ruling classes both in Latin America and in the United States; (e) by the doctrinaire and frequently simplistic attitude typically assumed in Washington in relation to Latin American problems; and (f) by the scant and diffuse understanding, by the people and the ruling classes in Latin America, of the gravity of the underdevelopment crisis and the urgency of basic reforms.

2. *The "relative stagnation" of Latin America.* Such stagnation is measured by the insufficient average rate of growth, a problem which evidently has roots that are much older and more widespread than the mere lack of success of the Alliance. In fact, even if the program had not declined from the height of the ambitions of Punta del Este, still it would be unreasonable to expect, during the initial phase of its implementation, a dramatic improvement of the general economic indexes.

Between March 13, 1961, and February 28, 1962, the total assistance to Latin America within the Alliance for Progress amounted to $1,029,-576,000. Between the former date and June 30, 1962, aid amounted to $1,517,300,000, including portions contracted for, but not actually disbursed.

The following were the main achievements during the first year of the Alliance:

1. Bolivia, Mexico, Chile, and Colombia completed their national plans for development.

2. Chile, Panama, Honduras, and Guatemala enacted legislation dealing with agrarian reform.

3. Ten countries enacted legislation on tax reforms.

4. Programs were initiated in several countries, dealing with social investments intended for the construction of housing and water and sewer systems, the establishment of schools and medical centers, and so on.

On the other hand:

1. There was no significant increase in the flow of private capital into Latin America, while in some countries there was actually a considerable decrease in flow.

2. There was no increase in the flow of foreign capital, either public or private, for the financing of basic industrial expansion.

3. In the majority of the Latin American countries there was no implementation of agrarian, fiscal, educational, administrative, and other reforms explicitly or implicitly called for at Punta del Este.

4. Throughout the majority of Latin American countries, the prevailing attitude toward the Alliance was characterized by an expectation of magical result, followed by frustration and resentment, and, in some cases by paralyzing incredulity. Generally speaking, the expected attitude of enthusiastic integration, expressed in pragmatical and rational terms, did not predominate in the Latin American countries.

5. In Washington, the Alliance has never been interpreted—either among the bureaucratic circles which operate the foreign-aid machinery or within a considerable portion of Congress, the press, and public opinion—in the bold terms which had presided over its conception. Among those circles the Alliance still is just a new name for an old program of assistance, a lever at the service of certain short-range national interests.

The period of the Alliance's first year was taken here as an example somewhat arbitrarily, due to a greater wealth of available data. It is worthy of note, however, that the months following the first anniversary of the Alliance did not bring substantial modifications of the panorama described in the preceding paragraphs, nor do the results permit a more optimistic evaluation of the picture.

The Alliance as an Ideology

The Alliance for Progress pretends to offer an ideological basis for the economic and social development of Latin America. In a sense, this ideological base is negative. The appeal of nationalism and the various modalities of socialism, including the extreme case of Marxism-Leninism, with the support of the Soviet bloc or of China, would supposedly be minimized by the existence of a supranational set of ideas, rich in motivations and capable of preserving the basic values of modern capitalism, with sundry concessions to the collectivist conception—such as, for instance, the requirement of state planning for the economy.

However, until now the Alliance has not succeeded in attaining the status of an ideological nucleus. Several Latin-American statesmen and diplomats have insistently remarked that the implementation of the Alliance lacks the emotional aura, the quasireligious participation that characterizes the nationalist or the Communist behavior in confronting the necessity for development. It is possible that there are reasons for this absence. The limited objective of this study precludes other than a mere statement of the fact, aside from the comment that an ideology based on elements springing from a rational conception of the world, with emphasis on individualism and founded on highly organized and technified cultures, would have to meet, as it is meeting, the greatest resistance in underdeveloped countries. Such countries are detached, to a large extent, from the so-called "Western tradition," and have their own highly varied characteristics, always imbued with a less rational and practical vision.

The ideological appeals of the Alliance would be (a) the frontal attack on the problem of economic underdevelopment; (b) the quest for social justice through structural reforms; and (c) the maintenance and perfecting of democratic institutions. Its ideological impact, through the mobilization of these elements, is conditioned to a preponderating extent upon the concrete effects of its own implementation. We are close here to being drawn into a vicious circle; but it is worthy of note that only as social and economic transformations are produced can there be developed the indispensable decisive elements, probably expressed in varied forms in view of the diversity of the political and cultural environment in Latin America. Without these results, there is little prospect that the Alliance will ever surpass the stage of a governmental proposition, accepted opportunistically by some groups and classes and attacked by others.

The Alliance as a Diagnosis

As a diagnosis of the crisis in Latin America, the Alliance for Progress simply adds to Operation Pan America a new emphasis on the social strangulation to which the Operation gave passing mention, generally dealing with it by implication. The basic economic problem is the same as described in the fundamental documents of the Operation.

An analysis of this diagnosis would reveal possibly an excessive generalization of the characteristic traits of economic and social development. If it is possible and desirable to establish the general outlines of the crisis, without which it would be impossible to prescribe the therapeutics for its solution, it is necessary, on the other hand, to keep always in view the diversity of the national and regional conditions of Latin America.

The danger of generalization lurks behind its usefulness. It suffices to think of the differences in culture and mentality that exist between Spanish America and Brazil, for instance, or on the national rivalries between Peru and Ecuador, or between Bolivia and Chile, to perceive the complexities which an abstract conception of the Latin American problem can bring to the task of its solution.

The Alliance as Therapeutics

Also in its therapeutics the Alliance does not differ substantially from Operation Pan America, although it does add four accents: (a) on the need for social and institutional transformation; (b) on the importance of social investments; (c) on self-help; and (d) on the obligation of the Latin American countries to execute some economic, social, and financial tasks.

The fulfillment, at least in part, of these tasks was considered for some time as a prerequisite to the supply of outside resources destined to set in motion the modality of inter-American economic cooperation. This dangerous mistake now appears to have been corrected, and there is, in the United States as well, a general recognition of the fact that it is impossible to achieve reforms and present the desired results without some prior help.

In the sections to follow in this chapter, consideration will be given to certain fundamental contradictions of the Alliance for Progress,

The History of the Alliance for Progress

which have disturbed its implementation and limited its political consequences. This analysis constitutes, in some ways, a preliminary examination of the adequateness and effectiveness of the therapeutics recommended by the program.

Contradictions of the Alliance

Stability vs. Transformation, Reform, and Social Revolution

The fundamental presuppositions of the Alliance for Progress include the following:

1. It is necessary that there be a social transformation in Latin America.
2. This transformation can be effected through an evolutionary process, without recourse to revolution.
3. The rapidity of such a process can be great enough to prevent the outburst of interfering revolutionary movements.

These presuppositions may be valid, but they are not immutable; it is probable that they are becoming each day less adequate to the Latin American reality. There is also no doubt that four years ago, when Operation Pan America was launched with the same fundamental purpose as the Alliance, it made some sense to proclaim the inevitability of revolution. There is nothing more inappropriate than a static view of Latin America as is implicit in the thought of certain statesmen and high officials of the industrialized world, when they suggest, for instance, that the strengthening of the European Common Market during the next few years will provide new and generous springheads of resources for a decisive impulse in the Alliance.

It is not an empty metaphor to affirm that the Alliance began a few minutes before midnight. Really, in a certain way, the Alliance is anachronistic and should have been set up simultaneously with the Marshall Plan, and even possibly before it.

To force the United States to recognize the Hemispheric need, the international circumstances had to impart the greatest gravity to the Latin American crisis. As we have previously seen, Brazil's cry in 1958 and the chorus of the two following years only elicited a tactical and, to a certain extent, evasive response. The role of the Cuban revolution as a catalyzer of United States attention cannot be lightly dismissed.

To expect, on the other hand, that more vigorous and defined effort should have been started by Latin America toward the unriddling of its problems is to show a complete lack of understanding of the Latin

American crisis. This mistaken view occurs rather frequently in the United States and in the industrialized countries of Europe. Its proponents seem unaware of the paradox—if the underdeveloped nations could show certain ideal characteristics of behavior, they would be proving in this way that they had progressed beyond the condition of underdevelopment.

Reform as a Prerequisite vs. Reform as an Objective

A brief reference has already been made here to the circular reasoning, today partly abandoned, that structural reforms must precede the decisive efforts of the Alliance in the terrain of economic cooperation. There is certainly a contradiction in admitting the necessity for social and economic transformation in Latin America and for programming a bold plan to carry it out, establishing targets to be attained within ten years, and at the same time to demand prior achievement of such reforms or of a substantial portion thereof as a prerequisite for the implementation of the program intended to produce them.

Immediate Effect vs. Long-Range Effectiveness

In order that economic investments reach a considerable degree of effectiveness in the long run, it is necessary that they find an adequate institutional and social infra-structure. From this consideration the rule might be derived that an initial priority should be given to the preparation of this infra-structure. However, it is not possible, concretely, to unfold these two stages in terms of time. Practically speaking, social investments, and institutional reforms must complement simultaneous economic investments; the latter must be effected before perfect conditions of receptivity exist for the former.

From this contradiction results the problem of "necessary waste," ill-accepted by the grantors of economic aid for development. The theory of "reform as a prerequisite," to which we have referred, is derived from this disagreement, born of a fundamental lack of understanding of the characteristics of underdevelopment.

Economic Planning vs. Private Enterprise

In the Western industrialized countries there is a tendency to imagine that the rupture of the barrier of poverty in Latin America could be engineered after the manner of an industrial revolution, with characteristics similar to those of the rise of European capitalism. Thus, it is natural that those countries should be inclined toward a conception of the combat against underdevelopment that would include private enterprise as a fundamental element.

It is true that ever more-widespread acceptance is being given to the phaseological conception of democratic-capitalistic economic development, according to which in the initial stages of the process of development of underdeveloped countries a substantial participation by the state in the economic life of the country is necessary. This conception is found especially among some university men and it has invaded, in various forms, the top administrative ranks. There remain, however, in various sectors of public opinion in the United States, samples of the old distrust of the role of the state as pioneer investor, as planner for development, and as agent for social transformation, notwithstanding the fact that in the U.S. the state is exercising such functions in a growing degree.

Another mistake is that which results from the expectation that exists, or has existed, in the United States of a swift and efficient execution of the national plans. This mistake also arises from the lack of understanding of what underdevelopment is, ignoring the fundamental fact that the reason for delays and inefficiency in planning is the very motive alleged as justification for planning.

A short reference should be made here to the problem of foreign private capital. It would be unrealistic to expect the contribution of such capital for the development of certain sectors of the Latin American economy, where violent emotional reactions would imperil the entire flow of private investments from abroad. In some countries such as Brazil, the public-utility services present a special problem, which can be solved through global negotiation.

The major part of private United States investment abroad is located in the developed countries. Of a total of $34.7 billion in direct investment, in 1961, $11.8 billion were concentrated in Canada and $7.7 billion in Europe, of which $3.5 billion were placed in the United Kingdom. The greater part of private capital in Latin America, totalling only $8.2 billion (less than in Canada), is invested in the production of petroleum and ores.

It is worthwhile to mention also one more vicious circle, one that has especially painful consequences. Monetary instability and political insecurity curtail the flow of private capital into certain countries. This circumstance, moreover, is self-aggravating, and the reduction of the flow increases the deterioration of the initial conditions of monetary and political instability.

Political Inspiration vs. Bureaucratic Inertia

The Alliance for Progress sprang from a politically inspired move of the United States, produced by the aggravation of international circumstances and by another movement of great innovating imagination—Operation Pan America. Its implementation, however, necessarily had to be entrusted to the bureaucratic classes of the United States and of Latin America, divorced from the original creative inspiration. The inevitable features of the bureaucratic conception thus serve as neutralizing elements against the original concept. In the dimension of the concrete instance, in which economic assistance is really valid, what meets the eye is the sluggish and legalistic treatment of the requests for financing.

A classic example of these difficulties is what could be called the "law of correlated shrinkage." In proportion as new sources of international financing are created, in order to meet the immense needs for development capital, the financing agencies tend to reduce their engagement, in the supposition that the new institutions will fully satisfy such needs. There occurs, then, with bothersome frequency, the paradoxical phenomenon of a growth in the opportunities to obtain financing, associated with an increase in the impediments to obtaining such financing.

The extreme complexity and disorganization of the United States foreign-assistance mechanism is another painful instance of the problems which hinder to an extraordinary degree the execution of the Alliance.

Annulment of Economic Aid through Losses in Trade

Of concrete importance toward the solution of the problem of foreign-currency financing of the projects for economic development in Latin America is the growth of the revenues in foreign currency, which can be obtained by increases in exports—the more natural alternative—as well as by amplification of the programs of economic assistance. The truth is, however, that there has been a trend toward neutralization of the benefits of economic assistance through commercial losses resulting from deterioration of the terms of trade. For instance, between 1953 and 1961 the average weighted value of Latin American exports to the

United States (except the special cases of Cuba and Venezuela) declined by some 20 percent while the equivalent price index for Latin American imports rose by 10 percent.

In the past two years, a period embracing the signature of the Act of Bogota and the launching of the Alliance for Progress, the price of sugar in the international market fell by 20 percent, cocoa by 26 percent, coffee by 8 percent, continuing a trend which began in 1955. If the prices of Latin American exports had remained at 1953 levels, the volume of such exports to the United States would have produced in 1961 an additional revenue of $1.4 billion, which is more than the total economic assistance received during that year.

In November 1962, Mr. Raul Prebisch commented, in Brussels, that due in part to the fall in prices of its exportable products, Latin America suffered during the past thirty years a considerable reduction in the regional per capita index of exports, namely from $58 in 1930 to $39 in 1960 (in dollars of 1950). Taking as a basis the period of 1950 to 1954, when these prices held to a relatively high level, ECLA estimated at $7.3 billion the loss of real revenue during the period 1955–1960 for the whole of Latin America, resulting from the deterioration of the terms of trade (in dollars of 1950–1954). During the same period, the net inflow of foreign capital corresponded to $7.7 billion, almost entirely in the form of interest-bearing loans. These figures are sufficiently dramatic to make comment unnecessary.

Trends in United States Public Opinion

The panorama of United States public opinion in regard to the Alliance for Progress is characterized by a fundamental negativism which assumes various graduations, from indifference to suspicion to clear opposition. Whenever support is forthcoming, it is generally lukewarm and reactive.

Today, at the same time that it is possible to detect a favorable feeling toward the Alliance among the high ranks of the executive power, among the more enlightened sectors of the two parties, in a small area of Congress and of the press, as well as in university and intellectual milieus, it is apparent that in the national opinion in general there are two predominating tendencies: (a) a desire for reduction in the amount of foreign assistance; and (b) a subordination of such assistance to national objectives to be specified with more clarity.

Both tendencies are likely to imperil the success of the Alliance. The first, for obvious reasons; the second because, when facing debate with those who criticize the essence itself of foreign assistance, final values are frequently confused with intermediate values—specific short-range objectives are taken as authentic national interests of the United States.

Recent symptoms of the discriminatory tendency are (a) Hans Morgenthau's study, published in the June, 1962, issue of the *American Political Science Review*; (b) the Chester Bowles memorandum; (c) the "Long Range Assistance Planning" of the Agency for International Development; (d) the general tenor of the Nineteenth Session of the Institute of World Affairs of the University of Southern California in Pasadena; and (e) the designation, by President Kennedy, of the Committee to Strengthen the Security of the Free World, which was charged, among other tasks, with examining the question of foreign aid.

Latin American Attitudes

As mentioned previously, the prevailing attitudes in Latin America toward the Alliance are also negative. They may be classified as follows: (a) expectation of magical results, generally followed by frustration and resentment; (b) immobilizing incredulity; (c) ideological opposition, from certain Marxist groups; (d) hegemonic opposition, based on defense of threatened interests; (e) opportunistic opposition on the part of some politicians; and (f) opportunistic adherence by other political groups.

As has been remarked earlier in this study, no ideological nucleus has been formed, which can create an idea-force to set in motion the frontal attack against the problem of underdevelopment. On the part of the Latin American leaderships, the Alliance is viewed generally as an assistance program which is broader than the previous ones and which, while producing new resources to finance industrial enterprises and minimize social friction, still is not supposed to require fundamental internal transformations.

As for the rank and file of the people, we would be unrealistic to suppose that they have, on the average, a clearer understanding of the objectives of the Alliance than their leaders do, although their distortions assume other shapes. Among the urban middle class in some of the more developed countries, and possibly even in some labor circles in those countries, there is some notion, albeit a rather imprecise one, of the aims of the Alliance. It is certain, however, that in countries such as Bolivia, Paraguay, and Nicaragua, the popular conception of the Alliance cannot but be an extremely precarious one.

Much concern is being evidenced by United States public opinion over the lack of support of the program on the part of the ruling classes in Latin America. In attributing to the state the inability to produce social transformations that are unattractive to the traditional elites—an assumption that is valid only for some of the countries in Latin America—it is the thought of some that "it cannot be expected that the ruling classes will commit suicide," in the words of Hans Morgenthau. From this consideration Morgenthau concludes that in many of the underdeveloped countries the option is not between democratic development and Communism, but rather between Communist revolution and non-Communist revolution, which, conveniently, he does not define.

Final Observations

Presidents Juscelino Kubitschek de Oliveira and Alberto Lleras Camargo have been recently entrusted with the extraordinary responsibility of indicating, objectively and with a constructive purpose, the problems which afflict the Alliance for Progress. The present study aims simply at presenting a synopsis of the history of this program together with an indication of some of its contradictions and difficulties, so as to serve as a preliminary contribution to the much ampler and deeper analysis of such problems. It may be expected, however, that an examination of such nature will outline, among others, certain specific problems.

Problems on the Side of the United States of America

1. The necessity of mobilizing United States opinion in favor of the Alliance, in order that the executive power may obtain the resources and the support necessary to implement the program within a useful period of time.

2. The necessity that the United States government learn to interpret its relations with the underdeveloped neighbors from the sociological viewpoint, stressing the long-range interests of that relationship, with pragmatical flexibility avoiding the pitfalls of a moralistic vision of international relations that insinuates aggression or a patronizing imperialism.

3. The convenience for the United States government of granting

decisive prestige to Latin American interests amongst the international financing agencies and other industrialized countries that are now suppliers of capital for development or may so become in the future.

4. The convenience for the United States government of employing all flexibility in the evaluation of the trade problems of the Latin American countries, and measuring the commercial policy of such countries within the general picture of their needs for external factors.

Problems on the Side of Latin America

1. The necessity that the elites perceive clearly the option confronting them—which they have to exercise with the utmost urgency—between: (a) concession and adaptation, or (b) chaos and revolutionary radicalism.

2. The necessity of mobilizing Latin American opinion for an energetic and prioritarian attack on underdevelopment, a mobilization which until this day has dealt largely with reforms.

3. The urgency of structural reforms.

4. The necessity of expediting preparation of national plans for development.

5. The necessity of complementing assistance investments of a social nature with massive industrial investments, indispensable for achievement of the initial stage in the process of autonomous development.

6. The necessity of restricting expenditures on armaments and military equipment, liberating resources for financing the social and economic development.

7. The convenience of laying emphasis on investment programs integrated regionally and sectorially, with sensible long-range effects, and on avoiding investments devoid of contextual usefulness.

8. The convenience of expediting as far as possible the economic integration of Latin America through the implementation of a common market.

One Problem Common to Both the United States and Latin America

1. The avoidance of the neutralization (that has until now occurred) of the flow of economic assistance, as a consequence of trade losses.

Index

Acheson, Dean: 17, 19
Act for International Development: 129–131, 139, 143. SEE ALSO Agency for International Development
Adams, John Quincy: 15
administration, public: 46, 47–48, 52, 55
Afghanistan: 137
Africa: 18, 19, 20, 31, 46, 72, 79, 116, 144
Afro-Asia: 26
Agency for International Development: criticism of, 132–134; mentioned, 94, 138, 142, 158. SEE ALSO Act for International Development
agriculture: taxation of, 7; neglect of, 58; protection of, 72; prices of, 114; production of, 114, 116
aid. SEE foreign aid
AID. SEE Agency for International Development
AID-EXIMBANK Coordinating Commission: 133
Alliance for Progress: creation of, 21, 54, 94; evaluation of, 29, 39–44, 54, 147, 148–153; compact of, 31; contradictions of, 40–42, 153–157; philosophy of, 91, 96, 146; funds for, 92, 93, 104; opinions on, 157, 158; mentioned, 13, 16, 17, 101
American Political Science Review: 134, 158
Anderson, Robert: 124
anti-inflationary programs: 113, 114
Arbenz, Jacobo: 29
Argentina: government in, 3, 49; oil enterprises in, 35; labor-union organization in, 116; monetary devaluations in, 118 n.; and Alliance for Progress, 148; mentioned, 140
Asia: 18, 19, 31, 46, 72, 91, 116, 144
authoritarian systems: 30

balance-of-payment: difficulties in, 7, 34, 78, 102, 117; loans for, 30, 93; deficit in, 119
Belize, British Honduras: 14
Bell, David: 134
Bentham, Jeremy: 56
Blackmer, Donald: 143
Blaine, James: 16, 122
Blumenthal, Michael: 149
Bogota, Columbia: 38, 123, 127
—, Act of: purpose of, 21, 31; subscribing to, 32; mentioned, 33, 34, 157
Bogota Charter: 127
Bolivar, Simon: 16
Bolivia: 35, 150, 152, 159
Boulding, Kenneth: on socialist and liberal, 55; and social sciences, 67
Bowles, Chester: criteria of, for foreign aid, 138–142, 158
Braden experience: 19
Brasilia, Brazil: 48
—, Declaration of: 125
Brazil: and Monroe Doctrine, 15; and International Monetary Fund, 30; and Alliance for Progress, 40, 148; and state intervention, 49, 88; civil service in, 52; development of, 56–60, 89–90, 92; political factions in, 56, 88, 89, 95, 96; coffee of, 77–78, 83–87; balance-of-payment problems of, 78; Gross National Product of, 89; imports in, 89; government of, 89, 90; social objectives in, 89, 96; inflation

in, 90, 93, 108; labor-union organization in, 116; and Operation Pan America, 126, 127, 128, 146; public utilities in, 155; mentioned, 26, 76, 145, 152, 153
British Commonwealth: 14, 73, 115
Brussels, Belgium: 157
Buddhism: 69
Buenos Aires, Argentina: 15, 16, 123
Burma: 144
Business Corps: 65

California: 15, 23
Camargo, Alberto Lleras: and inter-American systems, 124; and Alliance for Progress, 159
Canada: 58, 155
capitalism: 19, 27, 58, 69, 155
Caracas, Venezuela: 124
Caribbean: armed intervention in, 15, 29; resentment against United States in, 27
Castro, Fidel: 28. SEE ALSO Cuba; Cuban revolution
Central America: 10, 15, 23, 27, 29
Central American Common Market: 74
Chapultepec, Act of: 15
—, Conference of: 123
Charter of Punta del Este. SEE Punta del Este, Charter of
Chile: 116, 118, 140, 152
China: 151
CIAP (Inter-American Coordinating Committee for the Alliance for Progress): 148
Clay, Henry: 15
Clay Committee: 101
"Closing Remarks at the Conference on Inflation and Growth in Latin America": 114
cocoa: 73, 93, 103, 157
coffee: prices of, 34, 83; taxes on, 73, 103; loss of revenue for, 77–78, 84; importation of, 79; as export, 80, 84, 85, 86–87, 93; terms of trade of, 83
Coffin, Frank: 134, 142

cold war: 23, 26, 27, 129, 135
Colombia: coffee exports of, 87; mentioned, 3, 15, 23, 116, 141, 142
colonialism: 24
Columbia University: 53
Committee of Nine: 38, 148
Committee of Twenty-One: 126, 127
Committee on Loans for Development: 133
Committee to Strengthen the Security of the Free World: 158
commodities: prices of, 33, 77; approach, 73; export of, 76
Common Market, European: 31, 34, 43, 77, 79, 153
Communism: and nationalism, 24; threat of, 27, 123, 129; ideological ways of, 27, 151; appeal of, 28; in Brazil, 95
Communists: ideological pressure from, 18, 19; infiltration by, 23, 24; in Brazil, 56, 88; revolutions of, 97, 159
compensatory financing: need for, 33; funds for, 34, 72; purposes of, 73, 116, 118; programs of, 101
Confederation of Latin-Spanish Countries: 16
Conference of Punta del Este: 21, 28, 146
Conference of the Inter-American States: 16
Congo: · 88
Congress of Panama: 16, 122
conservatives: 96
consortiums: 141
Costa Rica: 23
cotton: 93
Council of Europe: 43
Council on Policy and Planning: 143
Council of the Organization of American States: 126
Cuba: 23, 36, 123, 157
Cuban revolution: 20, 21, 27, 28, 127, 153
cybernetic revolution: 66
Cyprus: 140
Czechoslovakia: 97

Index

Declaration of Brasilia: 125
Dell, Sidney: 105
Department of Economic Affairs of the United Nations: 105
Development Loan Fund: 33, 134
Dillon, Douglas: 21, 147
Dominican Republic: 23
Dulles, John Foster: 22, 125

Economic Commission on Latin America: (ECLA): 120, 157
Economic Cooperation Administration: 134
Economic, Social and Political Change in the Underdeveloped Countries and its Implications for United States Policy: 142–145
Ecuador: 152
education: importance of, 11, 58, 67; reforms in, 21, 54, 70; financing of, 33, 49
Eisenhower, Dwight D.: administration of, 19, 20, 31 n.; Newport Declaration of, 21, 34, 127; mentioned, 124, 125
Eisenhower Plan: 127, 128
Emerging Nations, The: 143–145
emulative mystique: 63, 69
engineers, industrial: 61–66 *passim*
"entreprenertia": 62
entrepreneurs: qualities of, 46, 51, 58, 63; national, 69; mentioned, 100
entrepreneurship: difficulties in, 8; advantages of, 45; as nonconventional input, 45, 62; encouragement of, 110
Europe: development of, 7, 58, 68; and United States, 15; keeping Soviets from, 17; and foreign aid, 31, 42, 73, 81, 92, 95, 104, 123; and International Monetary Fund, 30; investment institutions of, 147; mentioned, 25, 99, 120, 155
—, Council of: 43
European Common Market: 31, 34, 43, 77, 79, 153
European Economic Community: 72, 79, 80

Eximbank: 18, 94, 133
exports: primary, 4, 6, 7, 81, 102, 103, 111, 115; obstacles to, 9, 11, 58, 99, 111, 112, 115; revenues from, 9, 11, 73, 93, 94, 101, 103, 107, 118, 118 n., 121, 156; promotion of, 9, 76; expansion of, 10, 93, 114; of raw materials, 25; prices of, 31, 41, 72, 92, 94, 102; capacity for, 60; diversification of, 74, 103; increase in, 76; taxation of, 93, 116; decline in, 115, 116
Export-Import Bank: 18, 94
expropriation: 35–38

Felix, David: 31 n.
financing, compensatory. See compensatory financing
fiscal policies: 72, 120
fiscal reform: 22, 30, 54
Food for Peace: 94, 146
foreign aid: purposes of, 18, 31, 100, 101, 124; recipients of, 20, 71–72, 78, 84, 92, 93, 94; prerequisites for, 21, 22, 30, 99

General Agreement on Tariffs and Trade (GATT): 80, 104, 115
Geneva, Switzerland: 71, 80
Germany: 68, 74, 79, 80, 123
"Good Neighbor Policy": 16, 23, 146
Good Partnership Policy: 16
government: improvement of, 9, 11; intervention of, 48–52, 108; expenditures of, 119
Grace report: 101
grants: 17, 42
Great Britain: 14, 73, 115
Greece: 140
Gross National Product (GNP): 89, 92, 102, 140, 149
Grunwald, Professor: 115
Guatamala: 29, 150

Haiti: 23
Hamilton, Fowler: 134, 138
Harberger, Professor: 118 n.
Harbison, Professor: 61

Havana, Cuba: 123
Herrera, Felipe: on Marshall Plan, 124; mentioned, 43
Hirschman, Professor: and structuralism, 107 n.; mentioned, 53
Holy Alliance: 14
Honduras: 150
Hull, Cordell: 123

IAECOSOC (Inter-American Economic and Social Council): 92, 146, 148
IBRD (International Bank of Reconstruction and Development): 17
ICA: 94
IDA (International Development Association): 33
imperialism: 114, 24
imports: substitution of, 7, 9, 111, 112, 114, 121; protective policies on, 79, 103; prices of, 92, 157; amounts of, 93, 112, 115, 118; capacity for, 107, 111, 115; mentioned, 79, 89
India: 141, 142, 145
industrial engineers: 61–66 *passim*
industrialization: 3, 6, 7, 11, 25
industrial progressives: 24
industrial revolution: 66
industry: 58, 59, 90
inflation: toleration of, 6, 9, 25, 57; results of, 10, 36; types of, 30, 113, 115; curbing of, 30, 113, 114, 117, 119; views on, 90–91, 110–111; in Brazil, 90, 93; causes of, 93, 106, 109, 113, 119; mentioned, 50, 95
Institute of World Affairs: 93, 158
institutional reform: 29–32, 152, 154
Inter-American Bank for Economic Development: 127
Inter-American Committee of Presidential Representatives: 124
Inter-American Conference, First: 16
—, Fourth: 15
Inter-American Conference on the Consolidation of Peace: 16
Inter-American Coordinating Committee for the Alliance for Progress (CIAP): 148

Inter-American Development Bank: 21, 33, 127, 128
Inter-American Economic Agreement: 123
Inter-American Economic and Social Council (IAECOSOC): 92, 146, 148
Inter-American Economic Conference: 124
Inter-American Economic Conference of Finance Ministers: 33
Inter-American States, Conference of the: 16
International Bank of Reconstruction and Development (IBRD): 17
international development. See Act for International Development; Agency for International Development
International Development Association (IDA): 33
International Financial and Monetary Affairs, Committee on: 133
International Monetary Fund: stabilization programs of, 73, 80, 117; criticism against, 117–120; as symbolizing monetarists, 120; mentioned, 30, 31, 114
intervention: by the state, 12, 23, 46, 58; with arms, 23, 27, 32
investment: ineffectiveness of, 9, 10; public, 17, 34–38; private, 25, 34, 35, 54, 100, 129, 155; areas of, 35–36, 49; social, 40, 152, 154; government, 51, 57; importance of, 59, 71, 117; restraints on, 112; mentioned, 19, 50, 63, 111, 114
Iran: 142, 144
Iraq: 144

Jamaica: 140
—, Letter of: 16
Japan: 147
Joint ECLA-OAS Secretariat: 92
Joint United States Brazil Economic Development Commission: 19
Jordan: 135

Index

Kennedy, John F.: administration of, 21, 35; and Alliance for Progress, 17, 145; discussed, 142–143; and foreign aid, 158
Keynes, Lord: 100
Khrushchevian revisionists: 95
Kubitschek de Oliveira, Juscelino: and Operation Pan America, 39, 125; and role of Latin America, 125; and Alliance for Progress, 159; mentioned, 21

labor: 8, 11, 62, 67, 116
Labouisse, Henry: 134
land: reforms in, 21, 40, 70, 147; as conventional input, 62
Latin American Free Trade Association (LAFTA): 74, 115
Lebanon: 140
leftist movements: 95
Lenin, Nikolai: 24
Leninism: 151
Lewis, Arthur: 114–117
liberals: 58, 109
loans: purposes of, 10, 51, 130; problems of, 10, 17, 33; capital in form of, 25; amount of, 42; for balance-of-payment, 93; lower interest rates on, 147; mentioned, 33
—, public: 34
Long-Range Assistance Strategy: 138, 142, 158

Malvinas Islands: 14
managerial organization: 62–65
manifest destiny: 68
market: regulation of, 8, 33; flaws of, 58; access to, 71, 72; disruption of, 72
—, domestic: 74
Mao Tse-Tung: 24
Marshall, George C.: 17, 123
Marshall Plan: 10, 17–20 *passim*, 42, 43, 92, 123–124, 153
Martin, Edwin: 93
Marxism: 23, 28, 95, 151, 158

Massachusetts Institute of Technology: 142–145
Mediterranean: 17
Metternich, Prince von: 14
Mexico: international matters of, 10, 26, 28, 116, 150; and United States, 15, 23; mentioned, 16, 37, 123
Mexico City, Mexico: 92, 148
Mexico Conference: 149
Middle East: 144
military: 59, 71, 137
Millikan, Max: 143
mining exports: 7
Ministers of Economics and Finance: 80
Mollet, Guy: on Communism, 96
monetarism: 30, 106, 108, 117, 120
monetary stability: 30–31, 35, 60, 120
monopolies: forms of, 25; in oil industry, 35, 36; restraints on, 59
—, governmental: 49, 51
—, local, 5
—, private, 46, 49, 51
Monroe, James: 15
Monroe Doctrine: and inter-American relations, 13–15; purpose of, 122; mentioned, 17, 20
Montevideo, Uruguay: 123
Moreira, Marcilio: 25
Morgenthau, Hans: foreign aid theory of, 134–138; and development, 159; mentioned, 158
Muñoz Marín, Luis: on Alliance for Progress, 43
Myers, Professor: 63

National Consultative Committee on International Financial and Monetary Affairs: 133
National Planning Association: 104
nationalism: 3, 5, 23–26, 43, 56, 95, 100, 151
NATO (North Atlantic Treaty Organization): 20
neo-geopolitical approach: 20
neotraditional societies: 144
neutralism: 24, 26
Newport, Rhode Island: 127

Newport Declaration: 21, 34, 127
Nicaragua: 23, 159
Nigeria: 135, 141, 142
Nine Wise Men: 143
Nixon, Richard: 20, 124
nonintervention, principle of: 28
North Atlantic Treaty Organization (NATO): 20

OAS (Organization of American States): 28, 31, 80, 148
OEA: 143
OEEC (Organization for European Economic Cooperation): 43
oil monopolies: 35, 36
Omaha, Nebraska: 88
Operation Pan America: effect of, 21: and Alliance for Progress, 39, 152; launching of, 125, 153; objectives of, 126, 146; gains of, 127, 128; mentioned, 17, 38, 156
Oregon: 15
Organization of American States (OAS): 28, 31, 80, 148
—, Council of: 126
Organization of European Economic Cooperation (OEEC): 43
Organization of American States Compensation Fund: 73

Pakistan: 141, 142, 144
Panama: 23, 124, 140, 150
—, Congress of: 16, 122
Panama Canal: 23
Pan American Conferences: 122–123
Pan American Union: 16, 122
Paraguay: 159
parity: 33
Parliamentarism: 89
Pasadena, California: 158
paternalism: 6, 8
Peace Corps: 94
Peru: 20, 33, 116, 153
Petropolis, Brazil: 33
philanthropic syndrome: 72
Philippines: 145
Plan for Long Range Strategy: 138, 142, 158

Plano Trienal (Three Year Development Plan): 108
Plate River: 14
Platt amendment: 23
Point-Four: 19
Polk Corollary: 15
population explosion: 4, 111, 149
Populist Party: 88
Prebisch, Raul: 157
prices: fluctuations in, 7, 11; systems of, 8, 51, 58; of exports, 31, 41, 42; stabilization of, 31, 54, 89, 90, 100, 147; for imports, 42, 78; deterioration of, 77, 119; of food, 111, 112; levels of, 111, 118 n. 14
primary products: narrow range of, 4; bias against, 6; limit of markets for, 7, 72, 102, 104; prices of, 31, 33, 82, 94, 103; parity scheme for, 33; trade in, 72, 76, 82, 115; exportation of, 81
progressives, industrial: 24
public administration: 46, 47–48, 52, 55
Puerto Rico: 43
Punta del Este, Conference of: 21, 28, 146
—, Charter of: objectives of, 31, 32, 35, 38, 92, 146; mentioned, 33, 34, 40, 81

Quadros, President: 89

Reciprocal Assistance Treaty of Rio de Janeiro: 15
reforms: in the long-run, 39; in Brazil, 95, 96; and foreign aid, 99, 100; mentioned, 3, 25, 54, 58, 100, 140, 145, 150
—, educational: 21, 54, 70
—, fiscal: 22, 30, 54
—, institutional: 29–32, 152, 154
—, land: 21, 40, 70, 147
—, leftist: 88
—, social: 40, 70
—, tax: 21, 40, 70, 71, 140
reformists: 96
regional markets: 74
regulatory controls: 50

Index

religious patterns: 62
resources: creation of, 8; scattering of, 59; increasing of, 74; mentioned, 5, 10, 51, 68, 71, 146
revisionism: 24
Riddleberger, James: 134
Rio de Janeiro, Brazil: 16, 48, 115, 123, 125
Rio de Janeiro Reciprocal Agreement: 15, 23, 122, 123
Rockefeller, David: 65
Roosevelt, F. D.: 37, 123
Roosevelt, Theodore: 15
Roosevelt corollary: 14, 15
Rosenstein-Rodan, Paul: 143
Rostow, Walt: 5, 143
Russia: 14, 17, 137

San Salvador: 141
Santayana, George: 57
Santiago, Chile: 16
Santo Domingo, Dominican Republic: 30
São Paulo, Brazil: 148
Schmidt, August Frederico: 127
Schumpeter, Joseph: 6
SEATO (South East Asia Treaty Organization): 20
Secretary of State: 121, 125
—, Assistant: 93
—, Under: 21
Secretary of the Treasury: 147
shock mystique: 63, 69
Singapore: 140
Sino-Soviet bloc: 135, 151
Social Development Trust Fund: 94
socialism: 3, 19, 24, 58, 62, 70, 151
social patterns: 63
Social Progress Trust Fund: 127
Sophocles: 65
South East Asia Treaty Organization (SEATO): 20
Soviet bloc: 135, 151
Soviet Union: 14, 17, 137
Spain: 14
Spanish America: 152
stabilization programs: 108, 117-119 passim

state: 7, 25, 47, 58
State Department: 32
steel production: 50, 90
structuralists: 30, 106-119 passim
subsidies: 71, 80, 103
subsidy-pricing: 8, 48
subversives: 96
Sudan: 142
sugar: 157
supranationalism: 5, 26

Taiwan, Formosa: 145
tariff: 11, 36, 50, 80, 103, 123. SEE ALSO taxation
Tariffs and Trade, General Agreement on: 80, 104, 115
taxation: on specifics, 7, 79, 90, 103; of exports, 7, 93, 116; reforms in, 21, 40, 70, 71, 140, 147; for foreign aid, 42; types of, 49, 57, 71, 120; controls through, 50; administration of, 71; revenues from, 93, 114; of wealthier groups, 113; mentioned, 9. SEE ALSO tariff
technology: 4-11 passim, 51, 58, 67, 136
tensions: 13, 22, 23-24, 29, 39
Texas: 15, 23
Thailand: 142
Theobald, Robert: 66
Three-Year Development Plan (Plano Trienal): 108
totalitarian regimes: 32
trade: policies of, 34, 42, 72, 76; versus aid, 41-42, 71-74; terms of, 42, 95, 114, 118, 149, 156; and economic development, 77-87, 99; deterioration of, 101, 114; problems of, 102-104, 115
trade unions: 116
transitional societies: 144
transportation: 3, 36, 90, 120
transpositional illusion: 57
"Treaty of Political Sophisms": 56
"Trends in International Trade": 115
Trinidad: 140
Trotskyites: 95
Trujillo family: 30, 32

Truman Plan: 18
Tunisia: 141, 142
Turkey: 142

Under Secretary of State: 21
United Kingdom: 155
United Nations: 73
—, Department of Economic Affairs of: 105
United Nations Conference on Trade and Development: 71, 72
United Fruit Company: 23
University of Southern California (Pasadena): 93, 158
Upton, T. Graydon: 21 n.
Uruguay: 140
utilities: expropriation in, 36; subsidization of, 59, 71; rates of, 90; in Brazil, 155; mentioned, 120

Venezuela: 3, 20, 23, 140, 157

wages: 111, 113, 116, 120
Washington, George: 14
Western Hemisphere: 17
Western Hemisphere Parliament: 44
Western European Union: 43
wool: 93
World Bank: 31, 33
World Coffee Agreement: 80
World War II: 13, 15, 17

Yugoslavia: 136